The *Purrfect* Guide to Thinking Like a Cat

The *Purrfect* Guide to Thinking Like a Cat

Emma Milne and Karen Wild

THUNDER BAY
P·R·E·S·S
San Diego, California

Thunder Bay Press
An imprint of Printers Row Publishing Group
10350 Barnes Canyon Road, Suite 100, San Diego, CA 92121
www.thunderbaybooks.com

All notations of errors or omissions should be addressed to Thunder Bay Press, Editorial Department, at the above address. All other correspondence (author inquiries, permissions) concerning the content of this book should be addressed to
Amber Books Ltd
United House, North Road, London, N7 9DP, United Kingdom
www.amberbooks.co.uk

Project Editor: Sarah Uttridge
Design: Andrew Easton

Thunder Bay Press
Publisher: Peter Norton
Associate Publisher: Ana Parker
Publishing/Editorial Team: April Farr, Kelly Larsen, Kathryn C. Dalby
Editorial Team: JoAnn Padgett, Melinda Allman, Traci Douglas

Library of Congress Cataloging-in-Publication data is available upon request.

ISBN: 978-1-68412-285-1

Printed in China

22 21 20 19 18   1 2 3 4 5

CONTENTS

INTRODUCTION

Cats and humans have shared this wonderful planet for thousands of years. It didn't take long for cats to realize that humans can be quite useful to have around. With our big food stores and abundant rodents, we are attractive, and cats have learned that they are able to tolerate us. Our life with cats has been on their terms since they first realized this!

You may have heard the saying "Dogs have owners; cats have staff." Well, that is very true. It has taken a long time for us to come to grips with cat behavior, and many humans are still mystified by the things cats do. Cats evolved to spend most of their time alone. It can seem that they didn't develop complex communication. But cats are subtle creatures that live in a world of nuances most humans just don't notice.

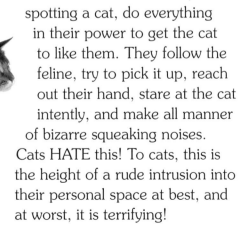

As a vet and cat owner, I often hear people say, "Argh, I hate cats, and yet they always come and sit on me." Let me tell you why. People who love cats enter a room and, on spotting a cat, do everything in their power to get the cat to like them. They follow the feline, try to pick it up, reach out their hand, stare at the cat intently, and make all manner of bizarre squeaking noises. Cats HATE this! To cats, this is the height of a rude intrusion into their personal space at best, and at worst, it is terrifying!

But consider the cat-haters. They are absolutely desperate for cats to stay away from them. They are petrified that, as is usual, the creature will make a beeline straight for them. They steadfastly avoid eye contact, they don't approach the cat, and they don't lean toward it. In fact, they totally ignore the animal. To the cat, this is the sweetest, least threatening kind of human ever encountered. And 30 seconds later, the cat is snuggled up happily on the cat-hater's lap! Freedom of choice is the key to happiness.

In the following pages, you'll discover lots more about the weird and wonderful world of cat behavior. With a strong focus on keeping your cat healthy as well as happy, this book will take you on a journey. These 501 tips begin with choosing the right cat. They will encourage you in kittenhood and take you through the grownup times, onward into those mellow senior years. If you already have a cat, you may start to notice things you'd never seen before. When you emerge at the other end, you're sure to be an owner worthy of a cat's hard-won love!

BEFORE GETTING A CAT

1. RESEARCH

Knowing the five welfare needs of animals (food, environment, health, sociability, and behavior) is an excellent and simple way to think about the care of any animal, including cats. Before you commit to owning a pet, you should research its needs and decide honestly if you can meet them.

2. NEEDS

Three of the welfare needs are physical things, such as needing a suitable place to live and the correct food, and these are usually easiest to get right. The other two can be thought of as happiness needs, and this is where many people go wrong, by not fully understanding their pet's requirements. The five welfare needs are as follows:

3. THE FIVE WELFARE NEEDS #1: FOOD

A cat is what's called an obligate carnivore. In the wild, a cat has to eat meat to get all the essential nutrients. Providing the right food for each time of your cat's life is very important. Fresh water should always be available as well.

4. THE FIVE WELFARE NEEDS #2: ENVIRONMENT

For most cats, this will be your house and yard or garden, and you'll need to ensure that there are lots of comfortable places for them to sleep. Think carefully if you don't have a yard. As you'll see, cats can get very stressed when kept indoors and can have behavioral problems and even some diseases as a result.

5. THE FIVE WELFARE NEEDS #3: HEALTH

Vaccinations, worm and flea treatment, neutering, illness, and injuries all cost a lot of money. Be realistic about money when thinking about pets. Cats can cost as much as $31,330 (£24,000) in a lifetime, and the average is around $15,660 (£12,000)!

6. THE FIVE WELFARE NEEDS #4: SOCIABILITY

Cats are solitary creatures by nature and don't need the company of other cats to be happy. In fact, many cats hate living with other cats and see them as a threat. Along with being kept indoors, living with other cats is a major cause of stress.

7. THE FIVE WELFARE NEEDS #5: BEHAVIOR

Cats do a lot of things that people don't like. They bring animals—dead, alive, or in pieces—into the home and sometimes put the animals into your shoes! Cats climb. They sit on work surfaces and scratch furniture. They treat us like slaves! You need to be prepared to love all these aspects of their nature.

8. HONESTY

If you already have a cat, think about these needs and ask yourself if there are any ways you could do better. If you're thinking about getting a cat or kitten, research all these needs really well, and be HONEST with yourself!

9. PRACTICE

It's not okay to deprive a cat of one of its needs because it's inconvenient. By learning all about your cat's needs beforehand, you can make the right choices about your lifestyle and whether a cat is the right pet for you.

10. LOVE

An animal can make life wonderful. Coming home to the welcoming chirrup from your cat can make the worst day all okay again. Remember that you need to be good to the cat, too. You need to uphold your end of the bargain!

11. ANCESTRY

Randomly bred cats from around the world can be traced back to eight geographic regions of origin: Western Europe, Egypt, the East Mediterranean, Iran and Iraq, the Arabian Sea, India, South Asia, and East Asia.

12. BREED HISTORY

Cat breeds are far more recent than those of dogs, who were selected for jobs that humans needed them to do. Most cat breeds are less than 100 years old. The humans who designed them focused mainly on looks and cosmetic preference, rather than useful traits.

13. DOMESTICATION

Even living alongside humans, cats have remained largely unchanged for thousands of years. It is thought that two main ancient lineages contribute to the cat breeds of today.

14. HOW CATS LIVED WITH HUMANS

Cats were brought into the human world to assist with vermin control, although it is thought that some cats, such as the Egyptian breeds, were also popular due to their sociability and tameness.

15. CATS IN HISTORY

While dogs were bred for certain purposes,
such as herding, cats already did what humans
needed. They offered companionship and
vermin-hunting skills, meaning they were
already as perfect as they are today!

16. EGYPTIAN CATS

Cats, known in ancient Egypt as the "Mau," were
an important part of ancient Egyptian society.
They were associated with the goddesses Bastet
and Mafdet and were routinely mummified. You
can still see ancient cat mummies in museums
to this day!

17. WITCHES' CATS

Historically, cats were associated with witches, and as a result, they
were often killed during the time of the Black Death, in the mid-
fourteenth century. This, of course, did not help keep down the
disease-carrying rodent population at the time!

18. CHANGES IN APPEARANCE

The cat's appearance has been changed the most in the twentieth
century, due to human selection. Our choices have sometimes had
disastrous consequences for the animal's health. Prior to this time,
only the tabby's stripes and coat were popularized.

19. EARLY LEARNING

Cats learn from everything around them, even when very young. Kittens that are not handled during the neonatal stage, or even those born to mothers not petted during pregnancy, may suffer. This can affect the kittens' reactions later in life. Gentle handling of alert kittens helps them learn not to fear human interaction.

20. INSTINCTIVE RESPONSES

These "knee-jerk" reactions are not learned: they are instant responses to a stimulus. For example, a sudden movement toward your face might make you blink. Cats are born with similar responses. Such a reaction is called an unconditioned response, meaning it is not learned.

21. LINKING STIMULUS TO RESPONSE

In the late 1800s, Pavlov, a Russian physiologist, pioneered the link between using a sound trigger and learning. B.F. Skinner, an American psychologist and behaviorist, then studied "operant conditioning," linking cues or commands to learned behaviors. Cats can learn quickly in this manner.

22. CONDITIONED OR LEARNED RESPONSES

Conditioned responses include many everyday examples of a cat's learned behaviors. A cat that is chased or held tightly by young children may quickly learn to avoid them or may learn to scratch and attack.

23. LEARNING WITH A PURPOSE

A cat learns based on what it finds important, what benefits it, or what causes the cat to be unhappy. This affects every aspect of a cat's life. If your cat has learned something, ask yourself what your cat was trying to achieve by this learning.

24. SURROUNDINGS

Cats are continually learning from their environment. The context of events affects their behavior, and the consequences of that behavior influence what they choose next. Cats will learn new skills, whether or not you want them to!

25. CONSEQUENCES. GOOD OR BAD?

The outcomes of choices can be reinforcing and rewarding, or they can be punishing. Cats may run, chase, and hunt with different consequences. They may seek or lose food, shelter, safety, or sexual partners. While cats seek to fulfill their needs with their behaviors, they will have differing preferences.

26. TRAINING A CAT

Manipulating learning through training teaches cats to work alongside humans. Normally, cats will avoid anything threatening, far more than they will seek reward. Punishment creates enormous stress in cats and is not a suitable training method. Reward-based methods are effective, kind, and preferable.

27. WHAT DO CATS FIND REWARDING?

This varies from cat to cat and is demonstrated by what the cat is looking to achieve. A cat will often avoid situations and seek out safety in high or concealed places. Strongly scented food may attract a cat; if so, the food may be used to good effect in training.

28. WHAT DO CATS FIND PUNISHING?

By definition, punishment is anything that causes a cat to reduce or entirely stop doing something. A cat is sensitive to nuance and may quickly fight back if it feels that something aversive is about to happen. A punishing situation can be as simple as a human's stroking the cat for too long.

29. LINKING LEARNING CHAINS

As with all learning, a cat links events together and can use these links to predict outcomes based on behavior. There is usually more than one behavior, known as a chain of behaviors, leading to a predicted outcome. Behavior chains can be very complex, based on the cat's previous learning.

30. DO CATS "TALK" TO US?

They certainly do, but we don't always understand them. All cat owners need to interpret their cats' signals correctly so that we don't trample the poor cats' feelings—or their tails!

31. LIMITED SIGNALS

Cats do not show the wide range of expression that we are used to from pet dogs. This means we may sometimes think our cats are tolerating things that they in fact heartily dislike.

32. INTEREST

When showing interest, a cat will focus its eyes intently. The cat may not move as it decides whether to approach or retreat. But just because the cat does not move away does not mean the cat is comfortable with the situation.

33. ESTABLISH SAFETY

Cats may wander seemingly innocently around the perimeter of a room, but they are checking whether or not to come any closer, and they are staying at a safe distance until that decision is made.

34. APPROACH

If the cat feels confident enough, the cat will come closer, tentatively, and will sniff ahead. The cat's head will raise and lower a little during this exploration.

35. EXPLORE!

Now it's time to have a look. The cat will examine the person or object. It's possible that the cat will jump onto a lap or into a box, if those are the options, but this is done to check out if the lap or box feels like a secure place.

36. SAYING HELLO

A cat that feels very comfortable will rub cheeks alongside your face, or rub its body alongside an object. The cat may bump its head affectionately underneath your chin.

37. TAIL UP STRAIGHT

It's easy to see if your cat's tail is up high in the air, which usually happens when it's approaching you. This is a signal of friendliness, greeting, and relaxation.

38. TAIL SIDE TO SIDE

If the tail is held out straight and moving side to side across the body, this can be a signal of aggressive intent. A cat's tail will thrash angrily, so you must heed this as a warning.

39. PUFFY TAIL

When the tail is held up and the fur is erect, this makes the tail fluffed out, often accompanied by raised fur along the cat's back. This puffy tail is a sign that the cat is very upset!

40. FACIAL EXPRESSIONS

Cats have flatter and more immobile faces compared with the faces of dogs, and as such their facial expressions can be more limited.

41. FLAT EARS

Accompanied by staring eyes, narrow pupils, and lowered head, flat ears are a sign that your cat is very unhappy and may behave aggressively.

42. ARCHED BACK

This is a defensive sign that may be accompanied by piloerection, where the fur on the back and tail is standing on end. The cat may leap and startle, or the cat may walk sideways while keeping an eye on the threat.

43. CROUCHING

When your cat is crouching down close to the floor with tail thumping, it's time to let the cat be. The creature is feeling defensive and needs time to calm down.

44. WHISKERS

When a cat has tightly closed whiskers pulled in against its face, this is a sign that the cat is scared. A relaxed cat holds whiskers a little more forward.

45. CAN I SOOTHE MY STRESSED CAT?

We often assume wrongly that we can calm upset cats by stroking or cuddling them. Many cats much prefer to be allowed to seek out a quiet place where they can groom themselves until they feel a little better.

46. CAT NOISES

Cats have a wide vocal vocabulary! These sounds can be used for mother-to-kitten communication, fighting threats, sexual approach, and of course cat-to-human chitchat!

47. MURMURING SOUNDS

Your cat's mouth is closed for these murmuring sounds, including the purring that we all love to hear. A cat uses these sounds for attention, greeting, acknowledgment, and enjoyment.

48. WHO CAN PURR?

All members of the cat family (*Felidae*) can purr, including lions, jaguars, tigers, and leopards, although these larger cats can purr only when breathing out.

49. PURRING SOUNDS
Domestic cats purr at a frequency of 25 to 150 vibrations per second!

50. TRILLS AND CHIRRUPS
These murmurs are the sound given as a cheerful greeting— just what we want to hear when our cats appear to meet us!

51. MEOWING
Many human languages contain mimicry of the cat's meow sound to describe this unmistakable vowel-laden noise. Usually, it's a friendly message to other cats and humans, but a hungry kitten uses this sound, too!

52. AGGRESSIVE NOISES
Yowling, growling, spitting, and hissing are all sounds that show a cat is very scared and stressed. It is trying to defend itself or is attempting to scare away a threat, without getting physical.

53. BREED AND BEHAVIOR

Cat breeds are becoming increasingly popular, as more people demand to choose the look of their cats, but the behavior and temperament of breeds is an important consideration. Many breeds are said to have serious, undesirable breed traits.

54. CHARACTERISTICS

Can breed dictate temperament as well as inherited disorders? Selective breeding and inbreeding have led some to suggest that some breeds have a pre-disposition to specific behaviors, many of which are problematic.

55. BREED DIFFERENCES?

Some cat pedigrees studied for breed differences have shown increased aggression toward other cats, aggression toward humans, marked differences in affection demands, and increased urine marking.

56. GENETIC HERITAGE

Research into behavior traits generally examines paternal traits, and it has been found that bold or friendly father cats tend to produce offspring with the same traits, as long as the kittens are correctly socialized.

57. PEDIGREE AGGRESSION

Compared with domestic shorthairs and longhairs, ragdoll and Cornish Rex breeds are seen as being less aggressive toward other cats, with the ragdoll showing less aggression toward humans. This depends on what the cats learn early in life, of course!

58. URINATION IN BREEDS
The Siamese and Sphynx are said to show lower urination marking compared with domestic short-haired and long-haired breeds, but there are gender and learned components that affect the outcome. Ultimately, this is not a useful observation when it comes to making breed choices.

59. PREDATION IN BREEDS
The Oriental is supposedly less likely to predate on birds than are domestic short-haired breeds and long-haired breeds, but of course, this will vary widely within individual cats. This cannot be used as a predictive guide.

60. CAN YOU CHOOSE BREED BEHAVIOR?
All cats learn from their surroundings, and there is no guarantee that choosing a breed means a certain set of behaviors goes along with this. It is better to look at the parent cats for clues.

61. HYBRID CATS

The Bengal, a hybrid resulting from breeding
the Asian leopard with the domestic
cat, and the Savannah, which is a
serval mixed with a domestic cat, are
common hybrids. Anecdotally,
Bengals show a high frequency
of undesirable behavior
traits, such as territoriality
and aggression.

62. BREED CHOICE AND CARE

Some breeds, such as Persians and exotics, need regular cleaning of
their eyes due to their flat faces, which obstruct tear flow. Be ready to
spend a lot of time cleaning these breeds. Long-haired breeds need
you to groom them frequently.

63. GENES

By their nature, pedigree animals are inbred to keep them looking the same as their breed. This means that their gene pool is relatively small, and in some breeds very small indeed. This, in turn, means that unhealthy genes can get multiplied. Many breeds tend to get certain diseases.

64. INHERITED DISEASE

Some breeds have much higher levels of inherited disease than others; so it's really important to speak to a vet and do extra research before you get a certain breed. You need to know how likely a cat is to get ill. Then, decide if you think it's fair to buy a cat, knowing that it could suffer from that problem.

65. HEART DISEASE

Some breeds, such as the Maine coon and the ragdoll cat, are prone to heart disease. The heart becomes very thickened, and the heart's inside volume gets smaller, so blood does not circulate properly. This is a serious and life-threatening disease.

66. KIDNEY DISEASE

Persians and some breeds related to Persians can have a high
incidence of kidney problems from birth. Screening tests can be done.
Always ask if the parents have been scanned or tested.

67. CARTILAGE PROBLEMS

Cats, such as the Scottish fold cat above, have been bred to have bent
and folded ears. The cartilage defect that gives them bent ears affects
all the cartilage in the body. This can cause crippling arthritis.

68. FLAT FACES

Breeds that have flat faces, such as Persians, can have many problems with breathing, dental disease, eye damage, and so on, just like flat-faced dogs. It's not ideal to promote the breeding of cats like this, so choose cats with normally shaped faces.

69. SHORT LEGS

There is now a breed of cat called the munchkin, much like the dachshund in the dog world, which is bred with very short legs. Having short legs is dreadful for a cat, as it can't climb or run. The condition also causes joint pain and arthritis.

70. HAIRY CATS

Cats with extremely long fur can really struggle to groom themselves and can be very difficult for you to groom. It's common for such cats to get matted, and this is very unpleasant for them.

71. BALD CATS

On the other end of the spectrum are the bald cats such as the Sphynx. These cats suffer from sunburn, cold, and are very prone to injury. Being bald is totally unnatural for cats.

72. TAILLESS CATS

Cats like the Manx cat have no tail or a very short tail. This is usually a sign of a spinal disease that is a bit like spina bifida for humans.

73. HIPS

Some cat breeds, such as the Maine coon, Persian, Bengal, Himalayan, Siamese, and others, can get hip dysplasia, so ask the breeder about screening tests.

74. OTHER DISEASES

Breeds like the Siamese, Burmese, and many others are prone to various diseases, such as asthma and gut problems. Always do your research before picking any breed, and find out about available health tests.

75. MOGGIES!

Thankfully, the vast majority of cats in the world are "moggies." This is a British term that means they are just cats—mixed breed, normally shaped cats. You can't go far wrong with a moggy. On the whole, moggies have fewer health problems than pedigree cats.

76. ADOPTION

Before you think about consulting a breeder, always consider adoption. You may think you'll never find what you're looking for in an adoption center because you're certain of what you want. BUT what harm can it do? There's no obligation to take any cat home, and you might just fall in love.

77. CIRCUMSTANCES

Sadly, there are thousands of cats all over the world that have been given up through no fault of their own. People get divorced, owners die, jobs get lost, and financial situations change. Many adoption centers have kittens or a waiting list for kittens, if you're desperate for a young cat.

78. GOLDEN OLDIES

Sometimes adopting an older cat can have lots of bonuses. The center is likely to have a good idea of the cat's temperament. You might also avoid the rather wild kitten years and drape climbing!

79. MATCHMAKING

Most good adoption centers are excellent at matching animals to your circumstances. By getting advice from an adoption center, you can be more certain of finding a great match for you and your family.

80. GOOD CAUSES

By adopting, you are contributing to a great cause. You are also immediately improving the life of that one cat, which will go from a cage to the comfort of a loving home.

81. JUST FOR US

Before you contact that breeder you found on the Internet, spend a couple of hours wandering the aisles of your local adoption center. You might be surprised.

82. BREEDER SETTING

A breeder with a large number of breeding cats and kittens is unlikely to be spending enough time with each kitten. Socialization may not have taken place, causing future problems in your home.

83. MOM

It's very risky to buy a kitten without seeing its mother and where it was raised. Ideally, try to find a kitten from a house or family situation similar to your own. This way your kitten is more likely to be used to a home like yours. For example, if you have children, look for a kitten used to kids.

84. MULTIPLE BREEDS

In general, it's best to stick to breeders who have a small number of cats of one breed, all of which are very well looked after. Breeders advertising lots of ages of kittens or lots of breeds are best avoided.

85. SYMPATHY

If you go somewhere and find a kitten living in a horrible, dirty place, it's human nature to want to save it. Resist this urge! You'll likely get a sickly kitten and will just reward a bad breeder by continuing his or her income flow.

86. BE BOLD

Good breeders should do all the health tests available for their breed. Don't be afraid to ask questions, and expect answers. Health test results should be openly available to you.

87. PET STORES

Kittens that were raised in or sold by pet stores are very unlikely to have come from an environment that is good for their early development, and you will rarely, if ever, see the mother. It's a high risk to buy kittens from pet stores, and only encourages them to continue selling more.

88. PET STORE ADOPTION

Some pet stores act as an arm for a local adoption center. If this is the case, you could consider a cat from there, but still be wary of the kittens, and check out the adoption center, too, to make sure it is reputable.

KITTENS!

89. PICKING A WINNER

Hopefully, you will find an adoption center or a breeder that makes you happy. You will still want to choose a healthy kitten, though, whether you settle on a pedigree or a mixed breed.

90. MALE OR FEMALE?

You may well already have a very clear idea about which sex to pick, or you may not be bothered. However, some diseases are more common in male or female cats. Also, neutering a female cat is more expensive.

91. HYGIENE

Hygiene is really important. Having lots of cats in one place definitely makes it more likely that you'll run into some diseases, such as cat flu and chlamydia. If the cats and kittens generally don't look well nourished and clean, and if they don't have healthy fur, walk away.

92. FOOD AND WATER

Can you see food and clean water available in the place where you choose your kitten? Even if the kittens are too young to have food yet, all nursing mothers should have access to good-quality food at all times. This is so they can meet the energy needs of feeding their litter.

93. VISITS

Good breeders should be happy for you to visit several times if you need or want to. Note that some may have age or handling restrictions when the kittens are very small to avoid bringing diseases in.

94. MONEY MATTERS

If the breeder expects you to hand money over and take the kitten then and there, be very suspicious.

95. PREVENTATIVE HEALTH

Vaccinations and worm treatment are very important for kittens and mothers. Depending on their ages, kittens may not have been vaccinated yet. Make sure you ask what the normal regime is. Ask to see proof of what's been given to the kittens and their mothers.

96. HEALTH

There are certain things you should look for in a kitten that are signs of good health, besides being well nourished. Check these things each time you visit your kitten to make sure they are consistently good:

97. KITTEN HEALTH CHECKS #1: MOVEMENT

Your kitten should be moving around normally, with no signs of lameness or other issues. If your kitten is always asleep every time you visit, this could be a sign of ill health.

If the breeder always hands you the kitten to hold, put it down so you can see how it moves.

98. KITTEN HEALTH CHECKS #2: EYES

Your kitten should have bright, clear eyes, unless it is still so tiny that its eyes haven't yet opened. If there is a lot of discharge or if the eyes are red or swollen, do not take the kitten. Runny eyes in kittens and cats are big signs of infectious disease.

99. KITTEN HEALTH CHECKS #3: NOSE

Again, runny noses and sneezing are bad signs in kittens. Cats and kittens hate having blocked noses, as they rarely breathe through their mouths. They also use their sense of smell a lot when they eat. It is likely that kittens with runny or blocked noses are not very healthy.

100. KITTEN HEALTH CHECKS #4: EARS

Ears should be clean and not smelly. Head shaking, scratching, and signs of wax or debris in the ears could be ear mites or infections.

101. KITTEN HEALTH CHECKS #5: COAT

The fur should be clean and shiny. Look out for scabs, black dots that could be a sign of fleas, and bald patches. Frequent scratching could also be a sign of problems. Cats and kittens are fastidious groomers. Dirty or matted fur is usually a sign that all is not well.

102. KITTEN HEALTH CHECKS #6: BOTTOMS!

As we said, cats are usually very clean animals. If you see a dirty bottom, this could be a sign of diarrhea, poor nutrition, or general ill health.

103. KITTEN HEALTH CHECKS #7: BREATHING

A cat's breathing should be silent. If you hear any wheezing, coughing, or other odd noises from a kitten, don't take it. If you hear an adult cat in the vicinity making noises, be equally concerned, as it may indicate that this is a house with infectious disease. Sometimes a kitten will start to show signs of illness only after it has moved to its new home, so a good preventative measure is to be aware of the adult cats that share the kitten's home.

104. NEW HOME

Bringing a new kitten into your family home is a huge responsibility. It is very easy to find kittens for sale. However, well-bred, quality kittens with good health and essential early socialization are hard to find. Prepare to spend several months searching for a kitten of good quality.

105. ADVERTISING

Advertisements that show kittens, online or anywhere else, always show attractive photos of cute litters. The advertising does not show any signs of poor care, which can affect the kittens' behavior. Kittens must be raised in a home environment if they are to settle into one.

106. "ACCIDENTAL" KITTENS

Often, people do not realize that their own cats are old enough to become pregnant or to father a litter. Kittens are often born into busy households. If healthy, these kinds of kittens may be good prospects as pets.

107. REHOMING

Ask about kittens found at your vet's practice or at a high-quality animal shelter. Check the mother cat's situation. You are looking for information about where the kittens came from, especially if they were reared by hand and fed by bottle.

108. HAND-REARED KITTENS

This kind of beginning can have a profoundly negative impact on the kitten's future behavior, including physical and emotional problems, for which you must be prepared if you decide to adopt one.

109. PEDIGREE KITTENS

Not only do you need to make sure you choose a breed that is healthy, you need to find a breeder who is rearing kittens that will make good pets. The kittens must be exposed to people and handled when alert within their first few weeks.

110. CHOICE OF KITTEN

Choosing from a litter is hard, so aim to see the whole litter at least three times before choosing. This gives you the chance to see the kittens when they are alert as well as tired. Look for signs of play. Do the kittens interact with each other and with people, or do they always shy away?

111. KITTEN TYPE

Ask the breeder to tell you about each kitten. Avoid extremes of behavior—for example, avoid a very quiet kitten or a very boisterous one. Try to pick one that has a bit of each quality.

112. ASSESSMENT

What kind of lifestyle do you have? If you live quietly, without many interactions, it may be that a shy cat is suitable. If your household is noisy and busy, with lots of people who are likely to want to stroke the kitten, choose a bolder one.

113. TWO KITTENS?

Sometimes, it may be easier for two kittens to grow up together than to introduce a young cat to an older one. However, there are no guarantees the kittens will get along when older, and it's very hard work!

114. ASK QUESTIONS!

What have the kittens experienced in their first eight weeks? What is the temperament of the mother? What about the father? Is there a breed disposition or behavior you should know about? Are the kittens kept in pens? Look for proof of the answers you are given.

115. DON'T BUY

Be prepared to walk away from any litter that makes you uncomfortable. This takes a lot of strength. However, it is rarely possible to fix a kitten that has been poorly bred and poorly socialized. You could have a cat for around 15 years, and with that kind of commitment, you should spend adequate time choosing.

116. KITTEN CHOICE

Ideally, your kitten should like to be around you and interact with you. This behavior has to be learned between the first three to seven weeks of life. Beyond this window of time, the kitten may tolerate contact but will find it very stressful.

117. KITTEN DEVELOPMENT STAGES

These rapid developmental levels vary from one kitten to the next. They are described in time-sensitive periods that may overlap rather than be clearly defined. A kitten's experiences during these stages can form its responses in adult life.

118. KITTEN DEVELOPMENT STAGES #1: 0 TO 2 WEEKS

The kitten is dependent on the mother's milk for nutrition. The teeth start to erupt, and the eyes open, but the kitten has limited responses to touch, warmth, or smells.

119. KITTEN DEVELOPMENT STAGES #2: 3 TO 4 WEEKS

Now the kitten's vision begins to play an important role. The kitten starts to walk but is a little wobbly still! The mother cat begins to offer solid food, such as live prey, as her kitten starts to wean, or stop relying only on her milk.

120. KITTEN DEVELOPMENT STAGES #3: 5 TO 6 WEEKS

Already the kitten can run for short distances. The kitten begins to kill prey and will relieve itself without needing stimulation from the mother.

121. KITTEN DEVELOPMENT STAGES #4: 7 TO 8 WEEKS

The kitten is nearly fully weaned from the mother cat. It will react to threats by startling, as an adult cat might, and will begin identifying potentially scary situations.

122. KITTEN DEVELOPMENT STAGES #5: 10 TO 11 WEEKS

At this point, the kitten can perform complex movements and activities. This is when you start to find your kitten running up and down the drapes!

123. KITTEN DEVELOPMENT STAGES #6: 12 TO 16 WEEKS

Now the kitten's eyesight improves even further and can spot movement very easily. You will notice the kitten pouncing on toys with more accuracy.

124. KITTEN DEVELOPMENT STAGES #7: 5 MONTHS

From this age onward and sometimes earlier, the kitten is considered to be at sexual maturity, but neutering is better done before this age to prevent unwanted pregnancy.

125. KITTEN DEVELOPMENT STAGES #8: 18 MONTHS

Your kitten has continued to develop but isn't considered to be socially mature until around this age. This immaturity may not affect humans but will be a big part of your kitten's interactions with other cats.

126. EARLY SOCIALIZATION

To prevent a young kitten from fearing the world, socialization should begin in a home as early as three weeks after birth, while the kitten is still with its mother. Exposure to gentle handling and the features of the human world should happen while the kitten is alert.

127. FAMILIAR AND UNFAMILIAR

Social contact must be established early, while the kitten is still learning to tell the difference between familiar, safe situations and unfamiliar, unsafe situations. It must vary a great deal so that the kitten can meet new experiences with confidence.

128. HABITUATION OR SOCIAL REFERENCING

These terms describe how a kitten gets used to its surroundings, learning that these places and events are part of daily life. For example, a kitten learns to ignore the noise of the refrigerator and washing machine just by being around them.

129. SOCIALIZATION

This step has multiple components. Kittens need to be exposed gently to people, other cats, and other kinds of pets especially, so that they become familiar with these variations.

130. OUTDOOR ENVIRONMENTAL FEATURES

Introducing outdoor sounds and sights is part of socialization. The kitten gets used to traveling in the car and hearing everyday noises without finding these situations frightening.

131. POSITIVE EXPERIENCES

When the kitten is exposed to exciting new situations, some places and events can can appear scary at first. Allow the kitten time to explore, and offer comfort and small pieces of food to increase feelings of safety and enjoyment. Keep sessions short and fun, giving the kitten time to rest.

132. TIMING OF SOCIALIZATION

The period during which kittens are most sensitive to learning about new situations and places is around 7 weeks of age. This critical period cannot be replaced, and it is crucial that the owner, or the breeder, takes responsibility for this social learning.

133. INFECTION RISK

Although kittens have not yet had their full vaccinations, their socialization must not be delayed. Ensure your kitten is not in contact with unvaccinated cats or other infection risks. But do not delay social contact. Simply observe the risks associated with disease.

134. PROBLEMS IN LATER LIFE

Kittens that are not socialized risk not being able to integrate as adults, causing them to fight and to suffer stress-related diseases due to fears, such as Feline Lower Urinary Tract Disease (FLUTD), immunosuppression, and skin diseases.

135. FAILURE TO SOCIALIZE

Without socialization, a cat's hypersensitivity to every new event and its fearful reactions create long-term stress. Remedial socialization is constantly required. There is no replacement for the early opportunity to learn.

136. IDEAL SOCIAL CONTACT

To give a kitten the best opportunity to learn about life, four or more people of all types must handle it. People of various ages, genders, and appearances must be able to play with the kitten.

137. KITTEN HANDLING

If you are going to invite people to handle young kittens, wait until the kittens are alert and want to join in, so that they can enjoy themselves!

138. HOW BEST TO PLAY

Have fun talking to the kitten, gently touching its body, holding the kitten, and playing together with toys, too!

139. MIXING WITH OTHER ANIMALS

Well-socialized kittens can play happily with other kittens and cats, if they wish, but also with other animals, such as dogs, chickens, and rabbits. Ensure the animals don't see each other as toys or prey, and don't allow them to chase each other!

140. CHILDREN ARE FUN!

Children can move quickly and be loud and shrill. They can play roughly and hug and kiss kittens in ways an older cat might not tolerate. Just as kittens have to learn human rules through early social contact, children must learn how to be sensible around cats, too.

141. CAT CARRIERS

Your kitten is going to need to be transported safely, so make sure this is a fun experience. Add treats inside the cat carrier so your kitten climbs inside and gets used to being lifted off the ground while enjoying the goodies inside.

142. COLLAR AND HARNESS?

If you are going to keep your kitten as an indoor cat, you will need to get it accustomed to walking with a special cat collar and harness when you take it outside. Be gentle, and allow your kitten to eat favorite treats at the same time.

143. TRUE CARNIVORES

Cats are true or obligate carnivores. In the wild, they have to eat meat to get all their essential amino acids, fatty acids, and vitamins. Adult cats need twice as much protein as adult dogs.

144. HUNTING

Cats are predators, and even if they are well fed, they may still hunt. Hunting isn't driven by hunger alone. It is a basic instinct. Cats will even stop eating a kill to chase something else if the opportunity arises.

145. TEMPERATURE

Because cats are built to eat freshly killed animals, they prefer food that's about body temperature. They won't mind room temperature food, but lots of cats won't eat cold food, such as food that's kept in the fridge.

146. KITTENS

Kittens' nutritional needs differ from those of adult cats because they need to grow as well as meet their everyday energy needs. Growing is hard work! Kittens reach adulthood at around 10 to 12 months of age.

147. WET OR DRY

If at all possible, you should feed your cat both wet and dry food. A cat can easily become hooked on textures. Later in life, your cat may need to eat wet food. For example, there may be bladder issues. You may need to offer dry food if finances get tight. If you get your kitten used to both, it could really help.

148. BALANCED

It's very important to feed complete and balanced kitten food. Home cooking can be done, but it's actually very difficult to make sure a homemade diet meets all the exact needs for growth and tiptop development. Ask your vet to recommend a balanced kitten food.

149. RAW

There is currently a trend to feed raw foods. This carries a significant public health risk for humans and can make your cat ill. There is a chance of bacterial contamination, such as salmonella and campylobacter. It's a high risk to feed raw foods.

150. ENERGY

Kittens need food with more energy or calories in it to ensure they have what they need to grow. However, it's still very important not to overfeed kittens, as obesity is very common nowadays.

151. PROTEIN

Kitten foods should have 30 to 50 percent protein for optimum health. This is measured on what's called a dry matter (DM) basis. Wet and dry foods can be compared directly only on a DM basis.

152. FAT

Fat is needed for energy, to help transport some vitamins, and also to provide fatty acids that cats can't make. The ideal range of fat for growing kittens is 18 to 35 percent. Don't overdo this, because your kittens could get too fat.

153. FATTY ACIDS

Fatty acids are absolutely essential for lots of reasons. In growing kittens, fatty acids are very important for the development of the brain and nervous system, the retinas in their eyes, and for optimal hearing.

154. MINERALS

Calcium and phosphorous are vital for growing kittens, and balanced kitten foods have very specific amounts of these nutrients. The balance is key. Kittens that are fed all-meat diets can have severe growth problems. Too much calcium is also a problem.

155. MILK AND WATER

After weaning, kittens and cats need only water to drink. Lots of people like to offer cow's milk, but this can cause bloating and diarrhea in some cats, so this is best avoided.

156. NORMAL EATING

In the wild, a cat eats 10 to 20 small meals a day, and its digestive system has evolved to accommodate this. Once your kitten is past the need for ad lib feeding, try to offer 6 to 8 meals per day. Timer feeders are very useful for this.

157. NORMAL DRINKING

Cats like wide water bowls, filled to the brim. This way they can avoid dipping their heads in the bowl, which makes them feel vulnerable. It also avoids their whiskers touching the sides of the bowl, which they find unpleasant.

158. WATER LOCATION

Cats in the wild don't usually drink water that is near their food because it could be contaminated by any dead animal they have found or killed. If you have room, place the water away from the food, and preferably offer several different bowls around the house.

159. SAFETY FIRST

Reactions to vaccines can happen, but they are incredibly rare compared with the number of vaccines given globally. Vaccinations have saved millions and millions of animal and human lives all over the world.

160. WHICH VACCINES?

The World Small Animal Veterinary Association (WSAVA) has a panel of experts who regularly review vaccination needs and safety. The WSAVA website has some really useful guidelines for owners, breeders, and anyone else who may be interested!

161. ESSENTIAL

Some vaccines are called core vaccines, and these are considered essential for every cat no matter where in the world they are. The non-core vaccines vary, depending on country and also the individual cat's lifestyle and risk.

162. MOM'S THE WORD

Mothers, or queens, as mother cats are sometimes called, that have been vaccinated will pass on some immunity to their kittens. This protects the kittens in the first few weeks of life, but it also stops vaccines from working. That's why vaccines start after the age of 6 weeks.

163. DEAD OR ALIVE

In general, there are two types of vaccines, dead or alive. They can also be referred to as noninfectious and infectious. Dead vaccines usually need repeating more frequently because they don't cause a big immune reaction.

164. FELINE PARVOVIRUS

Feline parvovirus (FPV) is an extremely serious disease with a high death rate. It causes various signs, such as diarrhea, blood changes, and weakened immunity. It's a very tough virus that lasts for years in the environment.

165. CAT FLU

This is what most people call the signs often caused by feline herpes virus (FHV) and feline calicivirus (FCV). These are the most important viruses, as they can cause death, especially in kittens. Common signs are runny eyes and nose. This can develop into pneumonia.

166. RABIES

Rabies is a massive killer of animals and humans in many areas of the world. The disease is spread when an infected animal bites another animal. Most commonly, this disease is found in dogs and bats. Rabies attacks the brain and causes many signs, including twitching, confusion, fear of water, and coma. It is nearly always fatal. You must follow the rabies vaccination rules of your country.

167. CORE

Every kitten should be vaccinated against FPV, FHV, and FCV. The first dose is usually given at 8 to 10 weeks of age and is then repeated at 12 and 16 weeks. A booster should then be given at 6 months or 1 year of age.

168. BOOSTERS

The FPV vaccine produces a strong reaction and needs a booster every three years. For FHV and FCV, the need depends on your cat's lifestyle. Talk to your vet. Your cat may need a yearly booster, or you may need to get one every two or three years.

169. FELV AND FIV

Feline leukemia virus (FeLV) and feline immunodeficiency virus (FIV) are also very important and deadly diseases. You can vaccinate for FeLV, and in a few countries, FIV. It's essential to test cats for these diseases so that we can try to eradicate these illnesses.

170. OVER-VACCINATION

If you have concerns about over-vaccination, talk to your vet. Sometimes you can have a blood test done to see if your cat needs a particular vaccine. It is important to vaccinate, because the whole population relies on it.

171. KEEP GOING

Your cat will continue to need booster vaccinations throughout its life. The frequency will vary depending on the vaccines and where you live.

172. TO NEUTER?

Neutering (spaying for a female and castration for a male) is often spoken about as a magic cure for behavioral issues, but this is rarely the case. Evidence points to some behavior changes from neutering, but rarely are all cases improved. Cats learn from their actions. Even if hormonally motivated, as happens in intermale aggression, these are still learned behaviors.

173. NEUTERING DEBATE

Never delay neutering, as your young cat can father kittens or become pregnant. Ideally, this is carried out at around 4 months of age, although some vets prefer to perform this much earlier.

174. MALES

Aggression is common
between intact males.
Without neutering, males
will wander much greater
distances seeking females.
Neutering helps to prevent
unwanted kittens. Humans
also report that the urine
of neutered cats is much
less pungent.

175. CASTRATION

Behaviors affected
by castration include
those influenced by male
hormones, such as spraying or seeking females, which are sexually
dimorphic behaviors. However, this is not guaranteed. Some males
perform these behaviors even after being neutered.

176. FEMALES

Spaying prevents your female cat from going into heat, characterized by yowling and frequent urination. However, spaying should not have other significant behavioral effects.

177. FIGHTING

Cats within the same household may compete for space, items, and other resources, such as food. This includes competition for attention from people. Fighting can be hormonally related if the cats are intact males, though they can be highly territorial even if neutered.

178. RELAX!

There's no benefit to a cat's ability to have a litter of kittens, and by not neutering, you are only adding to the number of homeless cats—of which there are already too many. And don't worry, your cat's personality is unlikely to change after neutering.

179. BENEFITS

In general, the health benefits of neutering and the elimination of the likelihood of unwanted kittens outweigh any other issues that may arise.

180. ROUNDWORMS

These are the most common worms in cats and kittens. Roundworm eggs can last in the environment for years. Cats get infected by accidentally eating the eggs or by eating rats and mice that have eaten the eggs. Different types of roundworms are found around the world.

181. SUSCEPTIBLE WHILE SUCKLING

There are always a few dormant larvae in a cat. When a cat becomes pregnant, these larvae wake up and go to the mammary glands. Virtually every kitten will get infected with worms when they suckle.

182. KITTEN WORMING

All kittens should be dewormed every 2 weeks from the age of 3 weeks until they are 9 weeks old. Then perform worm treatments monthly until 6 months of age.

183. FROM 6 MONTHS OF AGE

From the age of 6 months, kittens are wormed like adult cats. This should be done every 1 to 3 months for all types of worms, depending on how much the cats hunt. Talk to your vet about your individual situation.

184. TAPEWORMS

You will sometimes see tapeworm segments on your cat's fur or in the cat's bed. Fleas spread a very common tapeworm. Rodents spread other types. Tapeworm species vary worldwide.

185. VULNERABLE AGES

Tapeworms are usually a problem only in older cats, but if your kitten has fleas, you should also get treatment for tapeworms. Make sure any product you use is safe for kittens.

186. OTHER WORMS

Depending on where you live, your cat or kitten
may also pick up lungworms, heartworms,
hookworms, and even eyeworms! Find out
what's living in the area where you live.

187. WHAT TO USE

Be VERY careful about the products
that you use on cats. Some dog
products can easily kill cats. Ask your
vet what to use and how often you
should administer it—or how often to
apply it, in the case of spot-ons. Not all
products kill all worms, so ensure you have
everything covered.

188. MONEYBAGS!

Unless you are extremely wealthy, having pet insurance is a very good idea if it's available. Vets have state-of-the-art capabilities these days, and costs can be very high. It's very distressing to see people turn down treatments due to finances.

189. COVER FOR LIFE

Be very careful to read the wording of your insurance policy. Some policies say, "cover for life," but this means the life of the animal, not each condition. You may think you have adequate have coverage, only to find a condition is excluded after 12 months, so check your policy very carefully and ask questions.

190. MOGGIES VERSUS PEDIGREES

A moggy, or mixed breed, tends to be pretty healthy, but if your cat is hit by a car or gets a chronic condition, such as asthma or skin problems, the costs can very quickly escalate. Some pedigrees are quite prone to disease and should definitely be insured.

191. CANCELLATION

Think very carefully before canceling a policy or even switching companies. Anything you've already made a claim for almost certainly won't be covered by a new policy.

192. FRAUD

Please don't ask your vet or nurse to lie on an insurance form. This is fraud and is one of the biggest reasons that vets lose their practices.

193. MISCHIEF

Kittens are very good at getting into mischief. They are prone to injuries from certain activities, such as mistiming jumps, misjudging landing areas, or overestimating what they can do! They also like to play with stringy things.

194. WOOL AND STRING

A common cause of surgery, especially in young cats, is what vets call linear foreign bodies. Your kitten starts playing with a piece of string, swallows a bit, and then ends up swallowing a length of it.

195. THE LONG AND WINDING ROAD

As the string passes through the intestines, it becomes stretched along and stuck in certain places. The intestines gather into ruches and get blocked, and the string has to be surgically removed. This can damage long parts of bowel.

196. TAKE CARE

Many cat toys have string on them, and lots of people have string or wool sitting around the house. Make sure your kitten is never left alone with these items, or they can quickly disappear down the hatch!

197. DR. GOOGLE!

Vets and doctors the world over are now competing with Dr. Google! Please remember that speaking to your vet is the easiest way to be sure the advice you're getting is legitimate.

198. EAGLE-EYED

The more observant you are, the sooner you'll get to know what is normal for your cat or kitten. When you know what's normal, you'll quickly pick up on subtle changes and be able to act.

199. WHAT'S NORMAL?

Try to have an idea of your cat's normal appetite and feeding pattern, and how much or how often your cat drinks. If using a litter box, know what's normal for wee and poop, and how often the cat goes there.

200. EATING

Some cats like to graze, eating just a little at a time but often, while others badger you mercilessly for food. Increases in appetite could be a sign of diabetes or thyroid problems. A drop in appetite is often the first sign of illness, such as fevers, abscesses, or viral infections.

201. DRINKING

Cats originated from desert creatures and often don't drink very much, especially if they have wet food. Increased thirst is a very common sign of kidney problems and diabetes, among other issues.

202. VOMITING

Vomiting is serious because if an animal can't keep fluids down, dehydration happens very quickly. If your cat vomits frequently for more than 12 hours, you must see a vet. Vomiting very soon after eating food, even if your cat is alert, can be a sign of a blockage in the intestines. It needs investigating.

203. DIARRHEA

This can be pretty difficult to spot if your cats always relieve themselves outside. Watch for signs such as going out more often or dirty fur around their bottoms. If diarrhea is present for more than a couple of days, you should seek advice.

204. URINATING

Problems with urination are very common, most often because of stress, behavioral issues, or cystitis. If you see a cat straining to urinate but passing only drips or nothing at all, this is a medical emergency. Go to the vet whatever the time of day or night. Left untreated, the cat can quickly get kidney failure and die.

205. LUMPS

A cat that fights can get nasty abscesses full of pus that can be very painful indeed. Lumps can also be tumors, so always get them checked out. Try to get your cat used to being gently stroked all over from a young age, so you can notice lumps that fur might hide.

206. BALD PATCHES

Hair loss is normal, and many owners
are constantly covered in cat hair!
However, if you see bald patches,
with or without scabs, and itching,
get your cat checked out.
Hair loss can be a sign
of parasites, or it can
indicate allergies, among
other issues.

207. SNEEZING

Sneezing is unusual in cats and should always
be investigated. It may be a sign of something stuck in the nose,
especially if the sneezing starts suddenly. Chronic sneezing with any
kind of mucus coming from one or both sides should definitely be
checked. It could be a virus, polyps, or even tooth root problems.

208. BREATHING

A cat virtually never breathes through its mouth unless stressed or
very ill. Try to have an idea of your cat's normal breathing rate at rest
and when playing. If you notice coughing, wheezing, or open-mouth
breathing, go to the vet.

209. SMELLS!

Lots of things can change the way your cat smells. Watch out for smelly ears, skin, and breath. These can be signs of ear mites, infections, skin allergies, dental disease, and so on.

210. WEIGHT

Every time your cat goes to the vet, the cat should be weighed. If you have good scales at home, it's also worth weighing your cat every month or so. This is quite easy when using a cat basket. Spotting early changes in weight either way can be really helpful.

211. LETHARGY

Sometimes it's hard to tell if your cat is lethargic because some cats will sleep virtually all day! Once again, if you have an idea of your cat's normal activity levels and daily routine, you'll spot when something seems wrong.

212. EYES

Cat eyes can be damaged from fighting and also from infections.
Eyes can be permanently damaged if left untreated. If the whites of
the eyes are red or bloodshot,
if there's discharge from one
or both eyes, or if you see
swollen lids or squinting,
see a vet. Squinting or half-
closed eyes are usually signs
of pain.

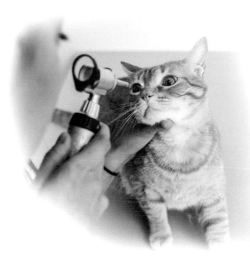

213. TWITCHES AND FITS

Any neurological signs
should be treated as an
emergency. Seizures can
be life-threatening. A head
tilt, weakness, knuckle dragging, facial droop, or twitching can be signs
of brain or spinal cord problems. Don't leave them too long.

214. BETTER SAFE THAN SORRY

Vets won't think you're stupid or wasting their time if you're worried
about something. It's better to be on the safe side, so if you're ever
unsure about something, go and see your vet. Lots of people have
later regretted that they didn't.

215. SCRATCHING

Scratching is a natural and important
behavior for cats. It keeps the claws
in good condition and is important for
territory marking and defense.

216. WHY DECLAW?

Lots of people don't like it when
cats scratch their furniture,
doorframes, and
carpets. The idea of
"simply" removing
the claws can seem
attractive and convenient
to some owners.

217. AMPUTATION

Declawing is actually not simple at all. It also involves amputating the
end bones of your cat's toes, to remove the claws fully. This is the
same as removing human fingers to the first joint.

218. SHORT-TERM EFFECTS

Short-term complications of declawing surgery include infections,
chewing the feet, pain, and lameness.

219. LONG-TERM EFFECTS

Newer research has looked at the long-term implications for declawed cats, and it's not good news. Declawed cats are more likely to bite people because they can't defend themselves. They have much more back pain, possibly because their gait is changed after the surgery. Long-term pain in the feet also causes aggression, behavior changes, and problems with the desire to relieve themselves in inappropriate places (such as the carpet.)

220. MUTILATION

Declawing cats is a mutilation that causes unnecessary suffering. It stops the animals from being able to behave normally and causes pain and distress. In many countries, declawing is illegal. If it isn't where you live, it is ill-advised to get it done.

221. DIVERSION

It's relatively simple to train cats not to scratch furniture and to provide places and surfaces for them to scratch to their hearts' content. Remember, it's not okay to deprive animals of one of their needs just because it's inconvenient for their human owners!

ADULTHOOD

222. OBESITY

Obesity is a growing problem in virtually all pets and in humans. Cat obesity is a huge issue. It can be very difficult to get weight off a cat. As we said in the section about kittens, if you keep your cat slim, this is by far the best thing to do.

223. BODY CONDITION SCORE

Body condition score, or BCS, is a great thing to get a grip on early. It's a way of describing how fat or thin an animal is. Some vets and nurses use a scale of 1 to 9, and others use 1 to 5. The middle number on each scale, a 3 or a 5, is ideal, as the higher the number is, the fatter the cat, and vice versa.

224. FALSE PERCEPTIONS

These days, many people are so used to seeing fat animals that those that are perfectly slim seem emaciated! We need to switch this perception back again and start seeing slimness as the right way to be.

225. KNOW YOUR CAT

Ask your vet early on to teach you how to assess BCS, and try to be always aware. Check your animal once a month, not every day. In this way, you'll notice a marked change more easily.

226. FEEDING AMOUNTS

As cats stop growing and also after they are neutered, their calorie intake needs go down. Some cats are very lazy and hardly seem to move all day. These cats will need way fewer calories. Always feed cats for the weight they SHOULD be. Ask your vet if you don't know what that should be.

227. HOW LOW CAN YOU GO?

If your cat is overweight or getting that way, be very careful about just dropping the ration more and more. Feeding tiny amounts of high-energy food can lead to protein, vitamin, and mineral deficiencies and also a very hungry, unhappy cat. Don't go below the feeding guide without vet advice.

228. DIETS

There are excellent light diets and weight-loss diets available, so talk to your vet about which one suits best. Feeding six to eight small meals and using wet food can also help a cat feel fuller. Timed feeders, as we said before, can really help.

229. EXERCISE

Whatever BCS your cat is, encourage exercise. Play with your cat, and have fun things to climb. You can hide food or use puzzle feeders to stimulate and exercise your cat, too. Access to the outside always helps as well.

230. DISEASE

Obesity causes lots of problems for cats. It makes it difficult for them to groom and stay clean; it reduces how much they can explore, jump, and climb; it puts strain on joints; it makes them more prone to bladder problems; and it's also a major cause of diabetes.

231. TIME TOGETHER

It's well established that slim animals live longer. By keeping your cat slim, you'll not only improve its health and quality of life, but you'll also get more years with your best friend.

232. GROWING PROBLEM

Diabetes is diagnosed more and more these days, probably because cats have become fatter, a bit like the human population. Diabetes in cats is very similar to human diabetes. It's called Type 2 diabetes.

233. INSULIN

Insulin is a hormone produced by the pancreas. It takes glucose out of the blood and allows it to be absorbed by the body in fat, muscle, and liver cells. The cells use insulin to make different things and to produce energy.

234. FAT CATS

As we said, diabetes is far more common in fat cats. Being overweight reduces the amount of insulin the body produces and also makes cells less sensitive to insulin. This double whammy means glucose stays in the bloodstream and can't be used by the body.

235. SERIOUS CONSEQUENCES

If left untreated, diabetes can be very serious. It causes weight loss, blindness, muscle problems, weakness, coma, and even death.

236. COMMON SIGNS

The most common early signs are increased drinking, urinating, and hunger. Unexpected or unplanned weight loss is also common. Cats with diabetes often look scruffy because their coats lose condition.

237. HOPE

If diabetes is picked up early, and you do as much as possible to manage it, many cats can go into remission.

238. TREATMENT

A multi-pronged approach is best. This includes a change of diet and weight loss if your cat is obese. Offering high protein and low-carbohydrate food, as well as small, frequent meals, can help. So can insulin therapy and home monitoring.

239. ADVICE

There is excellent advice on the treatment and long-term management of cats with diabetes on the International Cat Care website.

240. PREVENTION

As always, prevention is better than cure. Remember that overfeeding isn't kind, and it can even be deadly. Keep your cat slim, and the chances of diabetes and related problems will be lessened.

241. BLOOD SUCKERS!

Ticks are eight-legged creatures that suck blood. They are egg-shaped and range in size from around 0.04 inches (1mm) to 0.4 inches (1cm) in length. Adult ticks that are engorged with blood can be pretty impressive!

242. DROP IN FOR A BITE

Ticks don't fly or jump but get picked up when your cat brushes past vegetation or sits on it. Ticks will also drop from overhanging plants onto your cat and sometimes you!

243. HOT SPOTS

In theory, you could get ticks in a multitude of places, and you could also bring them home on your clothing, so indoor cats are not totally guaranteed a tick-free life. That said, some areas are much bigger hot spots for ticks. If you live near or in wooded areas and grassland, be vigilant. Also areas where deer or livestock graze tend to have higher numbers.

244. SPREAD OF DISEASE

Many ticks are important hosts for spreading disease. Some of the diseases they spread, such as Lyme's disease, are contagious to humans as well. Ticks carry different diseases, depending on where you live.

245. GET OFF!

There are many theories out there on how to remove ticks. You need to be sure that you don't leave the head buried in your cat because this can lead to inflamed and infected skin around the head. DON'T burn them out. It's ineffective, and you'll likely hurt your cat and get bitten!

246. HOOKED

You can buy tick hooks very cheaply. These clever little devices slide under the body of the tick, and a few turns bring out the whole wriggling creature. Ask your vet's office or local pet store if they stock the hooks.

247. VIGILANCE

Look out for ticks on your cats, and try to check your cats over when they come in from outside. If you find the ticks before they attach, they can do no harm. Aim for prevention, too. Not all spot-ons and sprays kill ticks as well as fleas, so make sure you know what you're using and that it's safe for cats.

248. YIKES!

Fleas spend most of their life off the cat, and for every flea you see, there are about 100 in the house! They can cause irritation in most cats and severe allergies in some.

249. BITES

Fleas bite to drink blood. A female flea needs nourishment for egg production and consumes up to 15 times her own body weight every day in blood. Imagine if we had to do the same!

250. SALIVA

It is a reaction to the flea's saliva that causes the redness where a flea has bitten. Most animals are slightly annoyed by this, as with a mosquito bite, but allergic animals can literally tear themselves to pieces. The self-trauma done by allergic animals can lead to secondary infections and very nasty skin damage.

251. CLUES

Flea dirt is a great clue to look for. Comb your cat's fur over a white piece of paper towel. If you see black specks, moisten the paper. Normal dirt will not change, but flea dirt, which is made of dried blood, will make a red patch on the paper.

252. FAVORITE PLACES

Fleas tend to affect some areas of the body more than others. If your cat has a lot of scabs or bald patches around the back end, neck, and groin, then fleas are high on the suspect list.

253. TREATMENT

Fleas are easy to kill and prevent but, especially for allergic animals, you MUST make treatment as regular as you are advised to do it. You also need to periodically treat the house to get rid of fleas and larvae in the environment.

254. DON'T BE ASHAMED

There is still a stigma attached to fleas, and many owners are mortified if a vet hints that their animals may have fleas. Many animals get fleas. It's just a fact of life and testament to what accomplished parasites fleas are.

255. MITES

Although less common than fleas and ticks, these parasites can still be a problem. Mange from mites is much less common in cats than in dogs but can still occur. Mange can be difficult to treat, depending on the type of mite. In some cases, mites cause intense irritation and skin damage.

256. LICE

Lice live on the skin of your cat and can cause itching but tend to be less irritating than fleas and mites. There are lots of different products available to treat them.

257. WORMS

Have a look back at the kitten section for a reminder of the different types of worms your cat might pick up. These will definitely vary, depending on where you live in the world and whether your cat hunts or not.

258. WORMING ROUTINE

Wormers don't prevent or repel worms, but they kill any that are there. Worming regimes vary, depending on the types of worms you're tackling and how often your individual cat may be picking them up. In general, adult cats should have worm treatments every one to three months.

259. BE SURE

There are now many
sprays and spot-on
treatments that are very
effective for prevention
and can cure these creepy-
crawlies, whether they are
inside or outside your cat. Always
check with your vet to see what is
safe to use, what the vet recommends,
and how often to use it.

260. SET REMINDERS

Not all treatments are effective against all parasites, so making sure
you have everything covered isn't always easy. Nowadays, there are
several apps available to coordinate control, and most vets will happily
send reminders. Embrace the new technology!

261. THREATS

Cats often live with other cats or have lots of cats around them in their territories. Being solitary by nature, cats fiercely guard precious things, such as space, food, and water. Rather than liking other cats, they usually see them as a threat, and this leads to lots of stress.

262. INDOORS

Cats kept indoors can also have much higher stress levels. They may be bored or frustrated. Many cats like to relieve themselves outside rather than in a litter box, and this can lead to reluctance to urinate and other bladder issues.

263. SUBTLE BEHAVIOR

Cats are very subtle with their behaviors, and lots of owners think their cats get along because they don't appear to fight, but in fact, their cats are silently bullying or being bullied.

264. SLEEP STRATEGIES

Some owners say their cats aren't stressed because they sleep all day. In fact, some cats will actually pretend to be asleep to avoid conflict.

265. LONG-TERM STRESS

Being stressed over a long term can cause bladder disease, gut signs like diarrhea, over-grooming, and coat changes. Some people call these cats "Pandora cats" because they can display a multitude of signs caused by stress.

266. EARLY DAYS

The environment your kitten is raised in can affect its whole life. Stress at an early age can make cats more susceptible to lifelong issues. We now know that a stressed mother's hormones can even affect a kitten in the womb!

267. SOCIAL GROUPS

Some cats will live together in the same social group. These cats will groom each other, rub against each other in greeting, and sleep cuddled up together. If your cats don't do this, they are probably not friends!

268. A HARD STARE

You may have a cat that sits near the food and stares at another cat. Even this kind of presence can be enough to stop a cat from getting to food or to a litter box. Just because a cat doesn't hiss and spit doesn't mean it isn't fighting.

269. LOOK AGAIN

Observe your cats with this new information. If they are in the same room, do they avoid eye contact and look in different directions? If they sit with you while you watch TV, are they always on opposite ends of the sofa? You might be amazed at what you've missed.

270. BLADDER PROBLEMS

When stress causes bladder changes, inflammation, high urine pH, and cystitis, cats can get crystals in the urine and sometimes stones. Male cats can easily get a blocked urethra and stop being able to pass urine. This is an emergency.

271. SURGERY

Cats that get blocked can go into kidney failure very quickly. Many cats will need surgery, hospitalization, and intensive care to nurse them through a blockage.

272. DIET

Diets that lower the urine pH have reduced protein and minerals to reduce the chance of crystals forming, and have fatty acids added to help inflammation. These diets can make a big difference to cats with these kinds of issues and can help prevent recurrence.

273. WATER, WATER, WATER!

Increased water intake is essential for stressed cats. Feed wet food if you can, and add water to it. Look into drinking fountains, and have several water bowls around the house. Anything you can do to encourage drinking will definitely help.

274. FREQUENT URINATION

The water going into a cat is important, but urine coming out is, too. Cats are great at holding it in. Offer litter boxes and access to the outside, if you can, to encourage frequent urination. This helps avoid urine stagnating in the bladder and crystals coming together to make stones.

275. EXTRA RESOURCES

Diet and extra water help, but if you don't tackle the stress in the house, your cats may have repeated problems. You should have more resources than cats. There should be one more litter box, feeder, water dish, and bed than you have cats. The items need to be all around the house, so your cats can access these precious things without conflict with other cats.

276. SHELVES AND LEDGES

Cats will be much happier if they can avoid contact with each other. If you have narrow passages that your cats travel along, think about providing furniture, shelves, and ledges so that one can go high while the other passes along the floor.

277. QUIET TIME

Think about places your cats can go if they want to be alone. You can even put microchip-reading cat flaps in internal doors so that a bullied cat is the only one with access to a certain room.

278. PHEROMONES

You can get pheromone sprays and plug-ins that make a huge difference to many cats. The pheromones mimic those of the mother or of territory marking and make the cats feel safer and more content. Don't worry, you won't be able to smell them!

279. SINGLE STRESSED CATS

Some cats that live alone get bullied or worried by cats outside. Think about installing a microchip-reading cat flap so that no other cats can get in to bully yours.

280. ROOM WITH A VIEW

Think about covering windows if your cat is feeling threatened by cats that can be seen outside.

281. CAT FENCES

Having access to the outside might be difficult where you are, but cat fences can really help. You can have a safe haven that your cat can't get out of, but that other cats can't get into either.

282. NEVER THE TWAIN SHALL MEET

Sadly, some cats simply can't tolerate life in a multi-cat house. You may sometimes need to consider rehoming cats. This may break your heart, but it can transform the lives of one and possibly many cats.

283. CURIOSITY KILLED THE CAT

There's a common saying about cats and curiosity. Cats are very inquisitive creatures and will get into trouble sometimes. Kittens are even more likely to try to go where they are not allowed. They can also squeeze into very small spaces.

284. AT RISK

Cats are certainly less likely than dogs to eat anything and everything, but this doesn't mean they are free from poisoning opportunities. Every year, hundreds of cats are accidentally poisoned, and sadly, many die.

285. ABSORBING POISONS

Cats will eat and drink odd things that you may not expect. They can also absorb some poisons through the skin. Cats are fanatically clean. They commonly get poisoned as they groom substances off their coats and then accidentally swallow the substances.

286. LETHAL LILIES

Lilies are extremely poisonous to cats, and even a leaf can be deadly if eaten. Cats can also become ill if they groom pollen off their fur. Lilies cause rapid kidney damage, which can be irreversible and fatal in some cases. Be very careful about houseplants and cut flowers.

287. HOUSE AND GARDEN CHEMICALS

Cats are commonly poisoned or scalded by detergents, such as bleach, washing powders, and so on. Creosote is also a big problem. Antifreeze tastes nice to cats and will be lapped up if spilled. Keep chemicals locked away, and clean up spills.

288. HUMAN PAINKILLERS

Human painkillers such as ibuprofen and aspirin can cause kidney
failure and gastric ulcers in cats, but paracetamol is absolutely
lethal. One tablet can kill a cat through liver failure. Never use these
medications on your cat, and keep them out of reach.

289. OTHER HUMAN DRUGS

Any human drugs could cause problems if eaten in large amounts.
Some antidepressants are quite tasty to cats, and overdoses can cause
vomiting, tremors, and diarrhea. Keep all medicines out of reach.

290. SPOT-ON FLEA TREATMENTS

Permethrin is a chemical found in lots of over-the-counter flea treatments for dogs. This is a big problem, because it's not uncommon for the treatments to get incorrectly used on cats or to find their way to cats through grooming practices. These products cause salivation, tremors, and seizures in cats, and they kill many cats every year.

291. RODENTICIDES

Cats will sometimes eat poisons meant for rats and mice, but more commonly, cats end up being poisoned by eating dying rats or mice that have taken these poisons. Most poisons for rodents cause blood-clotting problems.

292. OTHER PESTICIDES

Your cat can accidentally eat slug, snail, and ant killers. It's much more difficult to keep cats away from certain areas than you might think. Always make sure whatever bait you use for pests is pet-friendly.

293. ANIMALS

Depending on where you live in the world, your cat may catch or come into contact with poisonous animals, either through bites or stings. Try to know what your local wildlife is capable of and what signs to look out for.

294. COMMON SIGNS

Different poisons cause different signs, but many cause one or more of the following: vomiting, diarrhea, weakness, fits or tremors, salivation, excessive thirst or urination, drunken appearance, and abnormally fast breathing.

295. GO, GO, GO!

If you have ANY doubt in your mind that your cat has been poisoned, go straight to your vet, day or night. Many poisons have no antidote, but early supportive therapy can get many cats through the ordeal. Always take the potential poison with you, as this will help your vet enormously.

SUPER SENIORS

296. GROOMING

As cats age, they tend to get a bit stiffer, just like humans. This makes it more difficult for cats to groom, to reach those far-flung places, and to stay clean. You might need to help cats more as they age.

297. ARTHRITIS

A lifetime of jumping and climbing can take its toll on joints, and many older cats will have a little arthritis. You may need to put steps or furniture in place to help them reach their favorite eating or sleeping places.

298. LITTER BOXES

Older cats may not want to go outside to relieve themselves, so think about providing litter boxes if you haven't before. If you have boxes, you may find your older cats would prefer lower sides or softer sand, to make it more comfortable for them.

299. TEETH

Unless you've been very diligent and cleaned your cat's teeth for life, there's a good chance the cat's dental state will get worse. Talk to your vet about kibbles that can reduce plaque and tartar buildup.

300. ORAL HYGIENE

Your vet may recommend a clean and polish, and possibly extractions. Listen to this advice. Many animals suffer from gum pain and infections without showing obvious signs, and you often notice a new spring in their stride once their mouths are pristine again.

301.
NAILS

Cats virtually never need their nails clipped because they are very good at keeping them conditioned through scratching. As cats get very old, they scratch less often and less vigorously. Their nails can get thick and even grow into their pads. Keep an eye out for overgrowth.

302. SCRATCHING

Older cats with arthritis sometimes find it more uncomfortable to scratch on vertical scratch posts, because of the position they have to hold. Try offering horizontal areas for scratching instead.

303. BLOOD PRESSURE

Cats can get high blood pressure. This is rarely for unknown reasons and is more commonly because of other concurrent diseases. High blood pressure can cause blindness, renal failure, and heart damage. Your vet may include blood-pressure checks in senior screening.

304. COMMON PROBLEM

Kidney disease is one of the most common health problems in older cats. Too often, you won't see signs of disease until the majority of kidney function is lost, because the kidneys have a great deal of reserve.

305. SIGNS

The most common signs of kidney disease are drinking and urinating more than normal, and weight loss. In the later stages you may notice very smelly breath because of the toxins in the blood.

306. TOXINS

The kidneys are a major organ for excreting toxins and the breakdown products of food. When they stop working, these things build up in the blood and make the cat feel ill.

307. ANEMIA

The kidneys are also involved in the making of red blood cells. Cats with chronic kidney disease can become anemic when this function stops working well.

308. BLADDER INFECTIONS

Cats are descended from desert cats, and as a result, their kidneys are excellent at preserving water. Their urine tends to be very concentrated. As the kidneys get damaged, the urine becomes more dilute, and the cats can be prone to bladder infections.

309. STONES

Cats with kidney disease are
more likely to get calcium
oxalate bladder and kidney
stones. This is because the
kidneys lose calcium into the urine,
and this forms the building blocks
for stones.

310. SPECIAL DIET

Changing to a kidney diet is proven
to prolong life in cats with kidney
disease. These diets have, among
other things, lowered protein and
phosphorous. This reduces the
workload on the kidneys and slows
down the disease.

311. MEDICATION

There are several different medications your vet may recommend for helping with kidney disease. Luckily, these days many of these medicines are much easier to give than they used to be!

312. OUTLOOK

With the right diet and support, many cats can live for years after they've been diagnosed with kidney disease.

313. WHAT DOES THE THYROID DO?

A cat has two distinct thyroid glands that sit on either side of the windpipe, midway down its neck. They are usually small but very powerful. The hormone they produce controls metabolism and affects heart rate.

314. OVERACTIVE THYROID

When cats become hyperthyroid, it is usually because of a benign tumor that grows in the cells of the thyroid that produce the hormone. The glands produce more and more hormone, and the body works faster and faster.

315. THE LOW DOWN

Although hyperthyroidism (an overactive thyroid) is common in cats—having an under active thyroid is practically unheard of. The exact opposite is true in dogs.

316. SIGNS

Signs of thyroid disease relate to what the thyroid hormone does. Most cats lose weight, despite being ravenously hungry all the time. They can become grumpy or aggressive, their hearts race, they find it hard to settle down and sleep, and they can pace about as if they don't know what to do with themselves.

317. BLOOD DIAGNOSIS

Your vet may be pretty sure what is going on, based on the signs your cat is showing. In addition, your vet may be able to feel a goiter, which is the enlarged gland. The final diagnosis is usually made with a blood test that looks at the hormone level.

318. DON'T IGNORE!

It's not safe to leave a cat untreated. An overactive thyroid can lead to high blood pressure, blindness, heart failure, and uncontrolled weight loss.

319. TREATMENTS

There are four main ways to treat an overactive thyroid. All the options have pros and cons. Your vet will try to pick the one that best suits you and your cat, but make sure that you understand all your options.

320. MEDICATION

Drugs are commonly used to attack the tissue of the gland and to reduce the amount of hormone produced. Blood tests need to be done to get the right dose. Most often, medication takes the form of tablets, but in some countries a gel is available to put on the skin of the ear.

321. TABLETS

These drugs are generally cheap and easily available. On the downside, they can cause complications in a small number of cats. These issues include skin reactions, vomiting, and sometimes anemia.

322. SURGERY

Surgery can be done to remove one or both glands. It is not very invasive surgery, but all surgeries carry a risk. Your vet may want to stabilize your cat on medications before operating to make the process safer.

323. COMPLICATIONS

One serious possible complication of surgery is damage to some of the parathyroid glands—tiny glands that lie close to the thyroid glands themselves. These control calcium in the blood, and damage to them can be serious.

324. RADIOACTIVE IODINE

One treatment has radioactive iodine injected under the skin. It is taken up by the blood and into the glands, and the radiation kills the thyroid tissue.

325. HOSPITALIZATION

Only special centers are allowed to do this treatment because of the radiation. Normally, your cat will need to stay in treatment for up to 15 days, depending on the center, until the radiation is out of its system. A small number of cats will get low thyroid levels afterward and may need supplements.

326. LOW-IODINE DIET

A medical diet that is very low in iodine can be used to manage many cats. On the plus side, there are no side effects, you don't need to give medication, and you have to feed your cat anyway.

327. CONS

If your cat eats elsewhere as well, the change in diet may not be effective. A cat in treatment won't be allowed any other foods or treats. It's very important that you do not feed your cat other food if your cat is on thyroid medication.

328. CANCER

In some rare cases, the tumor in the thyroid gland is malignant. These cases have a much worse outlook. Your vet will be able to discuss options if this arises.

329. OUTLOOK

Many cats as well as humans do very well on a thyroid management program and have long and normal lives afterward. Please don't leave your cat untreated. Being hyperthyroid is very unpleasant at best, and at worst, deadly.

330. EARLY DETECTION

As you will have realized from lots of these health tips, there are many diseases that are best addressed early. There are also plenty that don't show signs until the disease is fairly advanced.

331. INTERNATIONAL CAT CARE GUIDELINES

This brilliant welfare organization has very good guidelines for many things. Their screening guidelines are often updated, and they give a clear guide to the best practices for picking up early signs of possible problems. Good screening includes the following:

332. SCREENING #1: ADULT SCREENING

When your cat is a young adult, up to the age of 7 years, you should arrange to have an annual health check, including weight monitoring and a full physical examination.

333. SCREENING #2: MATURE CATS

Cats are considered mature from 7 to 10 years of age, which is comparable to around 44 to 58 in human years. At this stage, cats should have annual health checkups, and the checkup should include a blood-pressure check as well as a urine sample, to make sure that urine is normal and to see how dilute it is.

334. SCREENING #3: SENIOR CATS

Cats are considered senior from 11 to 14 years of age, comparable to around 60 to 74 in human years. This age group should have a health and blood-pressure check anywhere from every 6 months to annually. A urine sample and a basic blood profile should be done annually. Blood and urine tests are excellent ways to detect disease early on.

335. SCREENING #4: GERIATRIC CATS

Geriatric cats are 15 to 20 or more years old. This is comparable to around 76 to 100 or more human years. These cats should have a health check every 3 to 6 months, blood pressure and urine tests every six months, and an annual blood test.

336. SCREENING #5: GOLD STANDARD

Of course, this is a gold standard. Not everyone can afford these tests, and not all cats are amenable to it all! The reason for stating the ideal number of health checks is that if you do as many as you and your cat can manage, you will be ahead of the game when it comes to prolonging your cat's life.

337. AGING GRACEFULLY

With old age come changes, and cats show many different behaviors related to their later years. They may take longer to move around, may sleep more, and may increase or decrease contact with you.

338. PHYSICAL AND BEHAVIORAL CHANGES IN OLD AGE

Hearing can diminish, and eyesight can be affected by medical conditions, such as high blood pressure. This can affect how cats perceive their world. Owners often notice physical changes, such as the cats' slower movements upon rising, but forget that the cats' emotions and behaviors are also impacted.

339. MENTAL AGILITY

Older cats are capable of learning new things but may need additional patience, for example, when learning new locations, if you have moved to a new house, or when getting used to changes in your lifestyle, such as a new pet or baby.

340. GROOMING

Grooming is so important to cats, but an older cat spends less time grooming and will need help from you to keep the coat in good condition. Be gentle and ensure your cat enjoys this.

341. HOUSE SOILING

An older cat may need to relieve itself more frequently or may not be able to access the litter box quickly, so ensure the cat can reach a place to relieve itself without having to climb or jump to this location. An older cat may avoid going outside in colder or wet weather, so add a litter box indoors.

342. A YOUNGER COMPANION?

You may add another cat to the family, but your older cat needs careful consideration. An elderly cat may not like being bounced on by a kitten! Your older cat may not appreciate having to share space, especially if it has not lived with another cat in the past or if it is usually a little timid.

343. OUT AND ABOUT

In retirement, some cats still love to hunt and roam, where others prefer nothing more than to lounge in a warm patch of sunshine. Allow your cat to find favorite places, and perhaps provide a ramp to climb to places once jumped to. Help your cat reach up and down in this way.

344. FELINE COGNITIVE DYSFUNCTION

As a cat's brain deteriorates with age, brain capacity can also diminish. Many medical conditions can also give the same symptoms, so get your cat checked at the vet as soon as you suspect senility.

345. CDS SYMPTOMS

If suffering Cognitive Dysfunction Syndrome (CDS), the cat may get trapped in corners, forgetting where the litter box is and relieving itself elsewhere. Your cat may not groom properly, may experience time disorientation, or changes to sleeping and waking cycles, and may sometimes exhibit aggression.

346. CRYING AT NIGHT

A common sign is for your older cat to cry at night or when you leave the room, yowling in distress. This reflects confusion about previously well-known household routines. This can disrupt your sleep, too, so do ask your vet for help.

347. MANAGING SENILITY

Aim to keep to existing routines, and look out for distress signs, such as yowling or sudden aggression. Your old cat will sleep very deeply and may not hear your attempts to rouse it, so go gently.

348. BRAIN FOOD

Some companies make foods rich in antioxidants, which help to reduce the signs of cognitive decline. Talk to your vet about whether one of these foods, or a dietary supplement, would suit your cat.

349. ACTIVITY CHANGES AND IMPROVEMENTS

Try enriching your cat's environment with activity toys, introduced gradually, such as puzzle feeders that force the cat to forage and use its brain to work out how to gain the food inside. If your cat enjoys your company, spend a little more time together.

350. SEVERE DEMENTIA

Some cats suffer severely with any change in routine, causing them to become more stressed, which in turn worsens the symptoms of cognitive decline. Try to keep routines as similar as possible.

351. DEALING WITH LOSS

Should your elderly cat pass away, be aware that your other pets need time and space for grieving. Prepare for pets to have extra support to recover from the loss. Provide nicer food, extra play sessions, and other activities in the early days and weeks.

352. INEVITABLE

We have amazing medical and surgical expertise nowadays, just as in human medicine, but sadly, death is inevitable. At least for our pets, we can offer a dignified end.

353. HEARTBREAK

Every owner who has ever said goodbye to a beloved pet will have felt the heartbreak that this brings. Many also experience feelings of guilt because it is their decision.

354. TALK

This can dwell in your thoughts for months, so make sure you talk to your family and friends as well as your veterinary team. It is an important job to help you through this time.

355. ULTIMATE KINDNESS

You make your cat's life as great as you can. Allowing your cat a pain-free death and an end to suffering is the ultimate kindness you can offer.

356. GOING PEACEFULLY

Many owners wish their cats would pass away quietly in their sleep. Sadly, it is very rare for natural deaths to happen this way. If you wait for this, you may well cause suffering to your cats.

357. KNOW WHAT TO EXPECT

Try to find out what will actually happen if and when your cat is put to sleep. Many owners dread or fear this stage, but if you know what to expect, you will cope much better because you will be at least partly mentally prepared.

358. HOME OR AWAY

Everyone should have the right to manage euthanasia as wanted or needed. If you'd like your cat to be at home in a familiar place with as many, or as few, people as you want, don't be afraid to ask. There are specific vets who will be able to accommodate your wishes.

359. SHOULD I STAY OR SHOULD I GO?

Some owners are desperate to stay with their pets at the end, but many wish to remember them as they were or simply can't face the prospect of staying. This is YOUR choice, and no one will think any less of you whatever you decide.

360. HELPFUL INFORMATION

There are a variety of online resources available to give you help and advice when the time comes. You can find out what will actually happen when your cat is put to sleep. If you're worried about staying, this may help you decide.

361. BURIAL

Depending on where you live, you may have the choice of burying your cat in the yard or garden if you'd like to. An owner may like to know that the cat is there, perhaps in the spot where the cat always chose to lie in the sunshine.

362. CREMATION

Almost every vet will offer a cremation service, individual or communal. An individual cremation is done on an individual basis, and you will have the choice of having your cat's ashes. If you choose a normal cremation, the crematorium will dispose of the ashes.

363. MONEY MATTERS

Like all things in life, death comes at a price. Talking about euthanasia costs, related billing, the timing of payments, and the costs of cremation can be very difficult for both you and your veterinary team. Discuss costs and settlement early on to avoid discussing these matters when you are upset.

364. COPING

Everyone grieves in different ways, and your vet will have seen every reaction, so don't feel self-conscious about being upset. It will take time to get over, so be prepared for that.

365. GRIEF COUNSELING

In many countries, there are specialist services to help pet owners through grief. Ask your vet or go online if you are struggling to come to terms with the loss.

366. REMEMBER THE GOOD TIMES

This may sound silly, but in the weeks and months afterward, look at photos of your cat when younger, talk about the cat with friends and family, and think about the funny or cheeky things the cat did. Laughter and happiness are great antidotes to sadness.

A CAT'S SENSES

367. DID YOU SEE THAT?

Cats use their eyesight much like humans do, to focus on objects of interest and to convey information to the brain, which interprets it all to get ready for action. However, cats' eyes are more suited to the purpose of hunting and tracking moving prey, or in some cases, moving toys!

368. LOW LIGHT VISIBILITY

Cats are crepuscular, meaning they hunt and are most active at dawn and dusk. They have six to eight times as many cells in their eyes for viewing objects in low light as humans do.

369. MOVEMENTS

A cat is much quicker to pick up movement, compared to a human. A cat's eyesight is ideal for spotting a mouse sneaking around the edge of the room, or a bird hiding in a tree, or your feet walking down the stairs!

370. CAN CATS SEE TELEVISION?

The recent introduction of high-quality digital images on television means that cats find it much easier to see the screen. However, their color blindness means they don't see the images in the same way as we do.

371. TASTE TEST

Cats have taste buds rather like our own, but only approximately 470 compared to our 9,000 or so. Also, the ability to detect sweetness is not as well developed in cats as in humans.

372. FOOD TEMPERATURE

Cats want food at room temperature or preferably as warm as live prey. A dish directly taken from the refrigerator is too cool.

373. TOUCH
SENSITIVE

Every cat likes different amounts of tactile contact. Some love to be stroked, and others find touch uncomfortable. Never assume that all cats enjoy petting.

374. PETTING

Allow the cat to approach you, and be cautious to observe body signals, such as the end of the tail flicking impatiently. A good rule is to stroke the cat for only a second or two, and then observe the reaction.

375. STROKE ME MORE!

If your cat enjoys your touch, it is likely to rub and push against you for more. Never insist that you continue if your cat does not do this. A cat is notoriously quick to tell you off if you overdo petting.

376. SOUND SEEKING

Cats have hearing that helps them navigate toward their goals, detecting and interpreting sound as it is funneled in the ears.

377. HIGH PITCHES

Cats detect many sounds that humans cannot, such as the scratching and squeaks of tiny vermin. This ability varies according to age, and loss of hearing in older cats or congenital hearing differences are common.

378. HEARING RANGES

Humans and cats have a similar range of hearing on the low end of their scales, but cats can hear up to 64 kHz in their upper range. This is a much higher sound than humans hear, and it's even higher than the range a dog can detect.

379. DEAF CATS

Cats that cannot hear still make use of the other senses and still make excellent pets and family friends. Extra care must be taken, as deaf cats cannot hear outdoor hazards, such as traffic. Hereditary deafness is often related to white pigmentation and blue irises.

380. A CAT'S SENSE OF SMELL

Cats' noses are renowned for their incredible sense of smell and their ability to detect and analyze many different scents, as well as differentiating between them. Cats use scent to determine territory, familiarity, and approachability.

381. UNDERSTANDING OUR CATS

Humans often fail to imagine how smells can help and hinder cats in our world, which is filled with a wide mixture of old, new, and different types of scent. Cats are strongly influenced by the scent landscape of their world.

382. NOSE CONSTRUCTION

A cat's nose is delicately constructed, and a cat must never be forced to sniff or contact strong aromas.

383. SCENT ANALYSIS

A cat's nasal cavity contains a rich supply of nerves, linking to the olfactory center in the brain. The vomeronasal organ, also known as the Jacobson's organ, allows the analysis of scent, primarily pheromones carrying information about emotions and mating.

384. PHEROMONES

These substances communicate sexual factors, such as the cats' maturity or whether females are in heat nearby, as well as information about marked territory or aggressive intent. Recently, pheromones have been artificially created in an effort to calm cats that are stressed.

385. CHARACTERISTICS

Cats have particular feeding habits, reflecting their natural instincts. They are not simply fussily rejecting the most expensive food you could find! Quite often, how often the cats eat, rather than what they are eating, is what matters.

386. EATING ALONE

Cats like to eat undisturbed. If your home has lots of cats, you need to keep plenty of feeding stations. You certainly need one per cat, with an extra one, too. This is true even if the cats all get along at other times!

387.
FINDING FOOD SOURCES

Help your cat fulfill natural hunting instincts by placing food into puzzle toys that can be foraged, or allow the cat to hunt around for hidden goodies. This also allows your pet to feed sporadically, rather than having one or two big meals a day—something a cat usually does not like.

388. LITTLE AND OFTEN

Cats use food to refuel and to get ready for their next activities. Piling too much food can put them off. You may worry your cats aren't hungry or don't like the food being offered. Be patient, and feed smaller amounts more frequently.

389. SELF-REGULATED FEEDING

Ideally, cats learn to eat when they are hungry and to not overfeed themselves. If they have highly palatable food at set times, they can often overeat and gain weight! Switch gradually to smaller, more frequent meals.

390. WHY DOES YOUR CAT PREFER BIRDS OR MICE?

Even with the most delicious cat food available, your cat always makes personal choices as to what is most enjoyed. A cat loves to hunt, which is why freshly chased, played with, and crunched-up mice may always be a temptation.

391. WATER

A cat's natural food sources are high in water content, including mice or birds! If you are feeding dried foods to your pet, you will also need to offer a source of water, and one the cat actually likes, too. Free access to drinking water prevents lower urinary tract issues.

392. WATER BOWLS

A solid, non-slip bowl is best. Your cat may prefer ceramic, plastic, or metal, so try out different types if you can.

393. FREE-FLOWING AND FRESH

Providing water in special cat fountains or running taps is better than in a stagnant bowl. Always provide one free-flowing water source per cat, plus an extra water source. Some cats enjoy a simple drink of rainwater!

BEHAVIOR AND TRAINING

394. CAT BEHAVIORISTS

A cat behaviorist analyzes learned behaviors in order to modify problems your cat may be having in daily life. Always employ a properly registered clinical animal behaviorist—usually someone your vet will refer you to.

395. HIDDEN SUFFERING

Even if your cat is not giving signs of unhappiness, take time to note daily routines and any situations the cat avoids. A cat does not readily show signs of stress, so learn all about your own cat's behavior.

396. UNDERSTANDING YOUR CAT'S NEEDS

This is all about learning what cats like to do. Cats need to have a choice whether or not to interact and do not show their discomfort readily. Make sure your cats are happy by designing their care around their behavioral needs.

397. BEHAVIORAL HEALTH

The health needs of cats extend beyond the physical. Their mental health is dependent on social interaction and on being able to express themselves freely. Cats do not give many signals, and so we may be completely unaware of the cats' stress until they become ill as a result.

398. THE OWNER'S JOB

A cat's behavior is the responsibility of the owner, who may push human expectations onto the unfortunate feline. This can interfere  with the cat's free expression of behavior. Allow a cat to behave as it wishes, such as by hunting. This may not suit all humans but is best for the cat's own welfare.

399. MIXING

Kittens naturally play as if they are chasing small prey, but cannot always judge whether it is a toy they are grabbing or your hand! Let them chase toys rather than fingers.

400. HUMAN FAMILIES

Owners can find kitten behaviors problematic as they can be a little rough and may damage furnishings or clothing. Never play rough with your kitten; confine it to a few, safer rooms at first.

401. INSTINCTS

Hunting, roaming, and exploring territory are normal cat behaviors, allowing the cat to engage its instincts. If suppressed, a cat can become distressed and will usually suffer unnoticed, leading to stress-related diseases. Remember that a cat can hunt for toys to spare wildlife!

402. BE KIND

Training methods, such as spraying water, shouting, or clapping your hands at a cat to stop it from doing things, are unnecessary and very stressful. The cat will learn not to trust people!

403. HEARING

Cats have sensitive hearing and must become used to everyday noises that may unsettle them. This means making time to familiarize them with sounds such as car engines, vacuum cleaners, and different types of music.

404. SCENT

Cats interpret scent in great detail, leaving humans uncertain why they may be reacting when nothing visible is apparent. Cats often indicate their scent response by rubbing their cheeks and sides along favored people and surfaces, as well as by scratching.

405. FREEDOM TO ROAM

Cats need plenty of roaming exercise, and this should be allowed as much as possible. Ideally, cats can explore the outdoor environment freely, enjoying everything in their local habitats.

406. NOT ENOUGH EXERCISE

Indoor cats may not be allowed to roam and may become overweight and stressed. Provide plenty of climbing surfaces at all heights, and encourage the cats to play as a means of encouraging fitness.

407. TRAIN YOUR CAT!

It is easy to teach cats some simple behaviors, such as climbing down from trees or getting inside before dusk, by calling their names and gently shaking a pot of treats and giving treats regularly. Your cats will learn to come to you whenever they hear the sounds.

408. YOU CAN TRAIN YOUR CAT!

Training is a means of directing your cat's behavior. It allows both you and the cat to meet a common goal, and it gives your cat an understanding of how to earn tasty food or attention without needing to paw at you.

409. POSITIVE REINFORCEMENT

Training based on positive reinforcement uses items or events to reinforce, or reward, desired behavior. If an outcome is rewarding, the cat will repeat the required behavior. If the outcome is unrewarding, it is less likely to repeat the behavior.

410. REPETITION

Cats are well aware of what benefits them. Trainers use repetition to ensure that cats have plenty of practice producing desired behaviors. Repetition must be consistent to avoid confusion. Training follows this format: The cat's attention leads to a cue or instruction from the trainer. When a desired behavior appears, the trainers provide markers. Next comes the reward.

411. ENCOURAGEMENT

With your guidance, all cats, even
tiny kittens, can learn the right way
to do things. If your cat is behaving
unacceptably, think of something you can
encourage them to do instead, such as
scratching a post rather than furniture.

412. CLICKER TRAINING

A clicker is a small device that makes a clicking
sound when the owner presses the button. A
clicker signals to the cat that a correct choice
was made, and the click is always followed with a tasty treat.

413. WHAT CAN WE TEACH?

A cat, especially an indoor one, needs plenty of enrichment activities. You can train your cat to touch a target to push a door open, or to come to you when you call. There is no limit to the useful things a cat can learn through training.

414. TIMING

Accurate timing in training is essential, so that the cat can link what the owner is trying to teach to the rewards. If the trainer is too slow, the cat cannot learn that a behavior is getting paid, so to speak, with food. The cat may not link the cue or signal with the desired behavior.

415. FRUSTRATION

Cats often have low frustration tolerance, so training must be made simple by using very small steps toward the training goal. Cats also do not like having treats removed at the end of a session. It's a good idea to finish off any training by offering the cats their dinners. That way, they can wind down gradually.

416. ESSENTIAL FOR WELFARE

Professionals agree that training is fundamental for your cat's well-being. This includes essential husbandry behavior, such as training to allow examination of the teeth. A cat will always be busy learning, and by training yours, you are simply adding extra quality to your pet's daily living.

417. STILL THINK YOU ARE IN CHARGE?

Ask yourself, how do you know your cat wants to go out? How does your cat tell you that it wants some affection? Do you know your cat has arrived because you hear meows calling you over? It's probable your cat is an excellent trainer!

418. NATURAL HUNTERS

In some cats, this instinct drives them to look for multiple opportunities to behave as the predators they are. They can decimate local wildlife populations, which not all humans appreciate. Cats love to catch prey!

419. PREDATORY TARGETS

Cats don't only aim to catch vermin, such as mice or rats. They will capture and kill birds—including chickens—and even baby rabbits, not always for consumption, but for the natural enjoyment and because of the instinct to hunt. Early socialization between kittens and other animals prevents this behavior, as the cats learn to see the other animals as members of the same species rather than prey.

420. THRILL OF THE CHASE

Seeking out potential prey, whether it's birds, rabbits, or rodents, can be exhilarating. Even if the cat doesn't catch a target, the hunt is rewarding. A cat may play with victims for long periods, until the creatures either escape or die.

421. FETCH!

Teaching cats to fetch means that even though they are allowed to chase after a moving object and hunt for it, they have been taught to return it to you. This is an enjoyable activity for both cats and owners in partnership.

422. TERRITORIAL INSTINCT

Cats value location very highly and often roam across a large area. This is a natural instinct and can often lead to fights between neighboring cats. Problems occur when cats are confronted and thus feel forced to defend a location. Indoor cats may not wish to share their space with others, resulting in fights.

423. AGGRESSIVE BEHAVIOR

A cat may choose to leave an area when a neighboring cat is around. However, a cat may defend the area, often silently at first, and then loudly yowling, growling, and eventually lashing out in an effort to chase the intruder away.

424. FEARFULNESS

Fears are completely normal reactions designed to keep every cat safe from harm. Alarming or scary events create an impulse either to flee or stay and put up a defense. A cat may freeze in fear, but it is most likely to flee or behave aggressively when stressed.

425. ANXIETIES

Anxiety occurs when a cat predicts or recalls a previously fearful event, even if it is not currently present. This creates problems when the cat generalizes a past fear to a wide number of similar situations. The cat may show all the physical signs of fear, attempting some sort of defense or escape.

426. PHOBIAS
A phobia develops when a cat's quality of life begins to be severely affected by fears and anxieties. Usually a phobia describes a specific stimulus, such as the presence of people, but as it progresses, it becomes impossible for the cat to function normally as a result.

427. TYPES OF FEAR AND PHOBIA
Cats may fear situations that have previously created pain or alarm. This includes sudden events that startled them, times when they were attacked by other cats, loud noises that hurt their ears, or times when they were left alone and panicked as a result of the sudden loss.

428. FEAR DUE TO LACK OF EARLY SOCIALIZATION
Commonly, cats originating from breeders or owners that did not socialize them develop fears and phobias. This is caused by their lack of experience at the crucial early socialization stage and is extremely difficult to resolve.

429. PLASTIC BAGS

Some cats show unusual interest in licking and chewing plastic bags, and these can be dangerous. Keep plastic bags tucked safely away, and use canvas or other reusable ones for general daily shopping.

430. WOOL SUCKING

This appears to be a misdirected nursing behavior but can lead to the cat's eating the wool or to ingesting long threads, which is very dangerous. It is common, especially in a younger cat, so be vigilant.

431.
DANGEROUS SUBSTANCES

As you will have seen in the common poisons tips, cats may eat or drink some surprisingly horrible things for such fussy creatures! Always make sure you keep any household chemicals well away from your cat.

432. BALD PATCHES

Patches may appear because of skin problems and sore spots, but can also be a sign that your cat is unhappy and is grooming excessively. Ask your vet to check for any illness, and consider whether or not your cat is experiencing stress.

433. PAWING FOR ATTENTION

Paws are great tools to gain your attention, especially if a claw is hooked into your sleeve! The cat learns it is impossible to ignore the gesture and thus continues, or amplifies the effort, until you simply can't say no to these demands.

434. ATTENTION!

If your cat is clawing at you for attention, or wanting to share your dinner, provide other games and activities suggested in this book to keep the cat busy at these times.

435. OUCH!

Did your cat scratch you? Maybe you stroked your cat for too long, or perhaps you scared it. Did you wake your pet up from a lovely sleep? Learn from our section on cat communication to make scratches less likely.

436. KIND HANDS

You will need to pick up your cat, groom, handle, and also play with it throughout its life. Make sure you are gentle when using your hands.

437. MANAGEMENT MEASURES

Keep your cat busy with toys, such as a fishing rod, to allow your friend to paw at something not closely connected to your hands. Rolling toys away from you for the cat to chase is another way of engaging in play without the risk of scratching.

438. SOLITARY CREATURES

Cats evolved to live independently, without needing to rely on others for survival. This is an important difference between cats and the other popular domestic pet, the dog. Many cats simply do not need companionship to be happy.

439. SELF-PROTECTION

Such incredible safety skills depend on the cat's judging when to explore or retreat. A cat is also superb at deciding where to sleep, even if this means occupying the couch while the dog ends up on the floor!

440. HELPING THEMSELVES

As with all pets, cats can be tempted by food left lying around at home, but remember that their incredible agility enables them to reach any leftovers with startling speed, even those you think were placed well out of the way.

441. FREE SPIRITS

Cats like to choose for themselves. You can cause your cats enormous stress by forcing them to do things they don't want. Even trying to make cats friendly by stroking them could lead to their dislike and fear of your approach.

442. CHOOSING TO WANDER

You might complain that your cat prefers the house next door because the neighbor is putting out food. However, your cat is choosing to find an important resource, which you may not give up as freely at home. Ensure that your home environment is as cat-friendly as possible!

443. NATURAL INSTINCTS

Cats seek spaces away from their own garden or yard to relieve themselves, usually in loose or softer soil. They like to bury their eliminations and will seek a place to comfortably scoop and scratch an area to go, covering it over once finished.

444. LITTER BOXES

These are used as indoor toilets but are often too small, meaning that the cat misses its aim or simply avoids the box. Make sure you buy the largest litter box you can find, and consider a box with a cover so that your cat can feel secure while relieving itself, away from the prying eyes of other cats, or even of humans.

445. LITTER SUBSTRATE

The litter box must contain a layer of cat litter, but these vary in type and texture. Some are clumping, which means they form a lump around any moisture. Others are lightweight, or in pelleted form. Your cat will have a preference, but do avoid scented litters, which can be unpleasant for the cat's delicate sense of smell.

446. COVERED LITTER AREAS

Some cats prefer not to be watched while relieving themselves, specifically by other cats in the neighborhood or in the home. Covered litter boxes allow for this. So does providing plenty of pots and other hiding places in the yard or garden, which can give cats additional privacy.

447. KEEP IT CLEAN

Some cats are fastidious about having an empty litter box and will not relieve themselves even if the faintest hint of a previous elimination lingers. Others simply don't seem to mind. Keep the litter box hygienic, and clean it as frequently as you can, to keep your cat happy and your home free of odors.

448. SEPARATE LITTER AREA

Never place your cat's litter box near a food or water source. Nobody wants to eat dinner next to the toilet! Keep the litter box somewhere quiet, in a place that is not near a main walkway.

449. CLEANING AGENTS

Avoid ammonia-based or other strong-smelling cleaners, as these quickly deter most cats and cause them to relieve themselves elsewhere. Even if the product says it is cat-safe, your cat may not enjoy the scent.

450. EASY ACCESS

Litter areas must be freely available because cats tend not to want to wait when they need to go. Providing more than one litter box resolves this issue by giving the cats more choice of location.

451. URINATION

Cats will often spray urine, not only as a marking of territory through scent, but also when they feel threatened. Ask your vet to refer you to a professional behaviorist for help with this.

452. RESTRICTED BOUNDARIES

More frequently, cats are kept indoors, without access to roam outdoors. This is due to the potential danger of predators, traffic, and theft, as well as the possibility of expensively bred kittens. Gardens or enclosures are provided, but they are wired off to prevent the cats from leaving the area.

453. TERRITORY

A cat loves to explore a wide-ranging territory. If this is not available due to indoor living, extreme care must be taken to provide the cat with other activities to maintain life quality.

454. STIMULATE

A cat without appropriate stimulation indoors may appear to sleep a lot. However, this is a sign that the cat is actually frustrated, depressed, and has given up. Try some of our fun cat activities instead!

455. HEIGHT ACTIVITY

Cats love to climb, so provide cat trees, which are designed for this purpose. Allow extra shelving to let them navigate your home. You can also provide plenty of beds in high locations, as many cats prefer an aerial resting place.

456. PRIVACY

Indoor cats don't get much opportunity to stay undisturbed, so they must be afforded hiding spaces, such as within cupboards, where they can easily enter and exit, or in extra cardboard boxes, which they can sneak off to. Never disturb them in these refuges.

457. FRESH AIR

Provide special mesh across windows, so that your cat can breathe in the scents from the outdoors, without your worrying about your cat's escape.

458. VARIETY

Indoor cats cannot seek out their own entertainment. You are responsible for providing a variety of toys, games, and other stimulation to help them remain happy and motivated.

459. FORAGING GAMES

Hide cat treats or dinners inside cardboard boxes, cat tunnels, paper bags, or even the cardboard from a toilet roll, so your cat can dive on these items and fish out the lovely goodies inside. This provides important stimulation of the cat's natural instincts.

460. CAT FISHING!

Feathers on a string attached to a small rod can be dragged around and flicked upward so that they seem to come alive for your cat to chase. The longer rod helps to protect your hands from overexcited claws.

461. FOOD TOSS

Instead of putting the food in a bowl, roll pieces of cat treats or food across the floor, so your cat can chase them. You can feed part or all of the cat's dinner in this way to really tire your pet out.

462. KITTY GRASS

Kitty grass, or cat-friendly herbs and other
plants, can be grown in trays indoors, using
special seed. Always check that the plants
you use are safe for cats, as some can
be toxic!

463. LASER TOYS

These toys encourage the cat to chase the
light that emits from them, as the light moves
quickly and is easily spotted, but they can also create a
lot of frustration, so be cautious!

464. CLAW MAINTENANCE

Cats stretch out their pads and scratch, usually with their front paws on vertical surfaces, to help keep their claws in good, sharp condition. Ensure your cats keep their claws neat by checking them regularly, especially as they age. The claws may need a little extra help from your vet at this stage.

465. MARKING LOCATIONS

Scratching also helps to mark territory, which explains why cats aim for similar locations to claw and pull in this way. Their paws stretch out, and their claws scratch at the surface, sometimes leaving visible marks but also plenty of scent.

466. UNWANTED DAMAGE

Unfortunately, scratching can cause damage to homes, including
tearing wallpaper, pulling carpet, or damaging furniture and upholstery.
Stay calm, and don't punish your cat for this natural behavior.

467. SCRATCHING POSTS

Provide a vertical post, specially designed for this purpose instead.
Ideally, the post should be enough for the cat to stretch out and use.
It commonly has a roughened rope surface as well. Some cats prefer
to scratch horizontal surfaces, so allow for both.

468. AGGRESSION TOWARD OTHER CATS

When a cat roams freely, it can be hard to know what to do if the cat comes home with ragged ears or other damage. There may be a neighborhood cat encroaching on your cat's territory. Or it may be that your cat is doing the bullying!

469. NEIGHBORHOOD WATCH

Look out for neighboring cats on fences or on trees, peering in, and provide your cats with plenty of cover in the yard or garden so they can come and go without easy detection. You may wish to mask windows if the outsiders are staring into the home, something all cats find very stressful.

470. TIMESHARE

You can reach agreement with your neighbors on when cats are allowed out. Perhaps yours likes to explore in the mornings and theirs, later on, at dusk. Agree to let your cats out only at these times, or look for a timed cat flap.

471. INTRUDER DETERRENTS

It's common to find other cats entering your own cat flap and dining on your poor pet's food, or spraying around it, for scent marking. Get a cat flap that is operated by a special magnetic tag or microchip that admits only your pet.

472. AGGRESSION TOWARD PEOPLE

A sufficiently stressed cat may scratch or bite humans. This can range from simply not wanting to be petted to active self-defense. This is a sign of extreme stress. Never force a cat into such a situation, and ask your vet to refer your cat for professional help.

473. MULTIPLE CAT HOUSEHOLDS

In houses with many cats, there are complex relationships between owners and cats, and among the cats themselves. Cats are not inclined to seek companionship, although some enjoy it at times.

Not all cats enjoy living with others, as cats are highly self-sufficient.

474. COMPATIBILITY

Ideally, littermates living in the same home should be compatible and learn to live together. Hormones, overpopulation, or simply housing a young cat with an older cat can lead to problems. Each cat must have its own bed, a space to rest undisturbed, plus there should be an extra bed.

475. COMPETITION

Cats may compete for food, but mostly locations. They don't understand the concept of sharing! Provide one food bowl, water bowl, litter box, and bed per cat, plus one extra. This is to ensure they don't begin a fight over access.

476. GROUP GROOMING

Happy companion cats will groom and wash each other (allogrooming) as well as curl up together. They often purr and seek out each other's company, not to knock one another off a perch but to share the resting space happily.

477. INCOMPATIBILITIES

Cats may not be compatible due to territorial or resource clashes. There may be a sense that the space is overpopulated. This is not easy to resolve without a clinical behaviorist's assistance, so ask your vet for a referral.

478. DOES YOUR CAT NEED A FRIEND?

Often, we wrongly assume that cats need a companion, or maybe we just want more cats! However, cats like to be solitary. Don't assume that friends are exactly what your cats want or need.

479. NEW CAT AND RESIDENT CAT

Aim to keep the resident cat's routine, and keep the new cat in its own room, where the resident cat doesn't usually go. Always provide each cat with hiding places to allow each one to move away.

480. RESIDENT CAT TIPS

If the resident cat likes attention, give plenty of treats and praise whenever the resident smells or sees the new cat. The first cat can come to learn that being around a new cat means fun interactions with you, rather than a worried owner who sounds anxious.

481. SCENT INTRODUCTION

Use a cloth to gently rub around the resident cat and a different one
for the new cat. Allow each cat to separately sniff the cloths and get
used to the scent. After a week or more at minimum, the cats may be
allowed to actually see each other, but use a stair gate or other barrier
first, so they can peep and hide if they wish.

482. GIVE IT TIME

It may take several weeks for the cats, or a cat and kitten, to get used
to each other's presence. Never force an introduction. If it goes wrong
due to your rushing them, you will harm their chances of living happily
in the future.

483. START EARLY

From early kittenhood, cats must become used to all kinds of people, especially children, in a way that is fun and enjoyable. Choose a kitten from a household that

can guarantee the kittens were regularly played with and exposed to people from all walks of life.

484. NEW BABY

Your cat will need time to adjust to a new baby. Allow the cat to sniff a baby-scented blanket before bringing your baby home. Keep the crib secure, and follow your midwife or doctor's advice on how to protect the baby, as a cat may decide to use the crib as a convenient resting place and the baby as a warm companion.

485. KIDS

Children behave in ways that may appear startling and unpredictable to a cat. Teach children to behave calmly around the cat and not to disturb your pet when eating or resting. Children are often taught not to hurt animals, but many will still hug a cat to show affection, which a cat finds highly threatening.

486. PLAY

Cats play by chasing one another, climbing around, clawing at toys, and pouncing and pummeling toys with their back legs. If they get to use humans as playthings, this can cause scratches. It may be time to invest in toys with which your cats can mimic these same behaviors without contacting human skin.

487. ROUTINES

Routine is important for a pet, as routines allow predictability and safety. A human household runs on routines, but the cat cannot always predict various celebrations, such as fireworks or parties. Give your cat a quiet, safe place to retreat to when routines change. Not every family cat wants to join in!

488. VISITORS

Visitors to the home may be very interesting for a cat, or they may cause a cat to become fearful and flee. Never ask visitors to greet your cat. If your pet wants to come and say hello, this will happen! Let the cat decide when, where, and whom to engage with. Don't take it personally if the cat would rather disappear.

489. ATTENTION

Human attention is rewarding for cats, but it can reinforce unwanted
behavior. Cats may learn to paw at you to gain attention or to get food
you are attempting to eat! Avoid punishing or paying attention to cats
at these moments. Encourage the cats to go to other locations, where
treats can be provided to enjoy instead.

490. EMOTIONS

Cats can be sensitive to the emotional atmosphere in human families.
It doesn't mean cats understand, but they will naturally feel unsafe
around conflict. At times of stress, grieving, or arguments, let your
cats leave the room if they choose. Don't be surprised if their behavior
changes at these times, too.

491. HOUSEHOLD RULES

Cats don't understand human rules, and it is unfair to punish or get cross at them when they are behaving naturally, even if that behavior involves climbing the drapes! Provide other areas for them to climb, or let them enjoy the trees outside perhaps.

492. TEAM EFFORT

Everyone who comes into contact with the cat must understand cat behavior and needs, such as letting the cat rest, allowing the cat to wriggle free when in need of a break, and even training the cat to come in at night.

493. WHO IS IN CHARGE?

It is helpful if one member of the household takes responsibility for ensuring the cat's routine is maintained. This is usually a responsible adult, but often youngsters make great pet caretakers if adults make time to teach them. Read them sections of this book!

494. CHILDREN AND HOUSEHOLD RULES

Kids make excellent caretakers for a cat, as long as the children know the rules. Put small signs around the house to remind them to let the cat sleep undisturbed, to use specific toys rather than their hands when playing with the cat, and not to hug the cat.

495. SET A ROSTER!

To make sure rules are followed, a roster will help the family share tasks, such as cleaning the litter box, ensuring the cat is fed little and often, playing with the right cat toys, and letting your cat rest when needed.

496. STAR CHART FOR YOUNG CHILDREN

Cats must learn that little kids are fun, not the loud and scary creatures that some cats, not socialized properly, believe children to be. Every time young children behave responsibly toward cats, give them stickers for a star chart!

497. RULES ARE RULES

If a member of the household refuses to follow the rules, simply prevent that person from interacting with the cat until he or she agrees to them. A cat doesn't want to live in stress and fear. Your cat will thank you for your care and attention to its needs!

498. SPEND TIME ENJOYING YOUR PET

After reading these tips, you may feel a little overwhelmed by the numerous things you could/ should be doing. But be sure to simply spend time just enjoying your cat for the lovely pet and companion your cat is.

499. LET YOUR CAT BE ITSELF

Although cats often do things we humans don't like, work out what you can live with. Cats will be much happier if they can live as naturally as possible. Cats like to be loners and are very self-sufficient, but they need our shelter and care, too. It's important to get the right balance.

500. COMPANIONS TO THE LAST

We are privileged to spend our time with cats, and they often choose to be with us, too. Cats come and go freely, the way they like to live, which often suits our busy human lives.

501. AND FINALLY

We hope you've enjoyed this little tour through the wonderful world of the cat. A cat can make the most fantastic companion and be your best friend in the world, but we have to live up to that friendship, too. Hopefully, these tips will help make you the best friend your cat can have!

Picture Credits

Dreamstime: 6 (Nelikz), 7 (Kucher Serhii), 8 (Anna Utekhina), 10 (Studio Barcelona), 16 (Nikolai Tsvetkov), 19 (Elena Butinova), 25 bottom (Nousha), 37 (Anna Utekhina), 41 (Anucha Pongpatimeth), 42 (Czanner), 58 bottom (Photodeti), 98 bottom (Anna Utekhina), 99 (Linn Currie), 110 (Cynoclub), 117 (Erik Lam), 118 bottom (Nelikz), 119 (Anna Utekhina), 120 (Sarah Fields), 121 top (Dimakp), 121 bottom (Svetlana Gladkova), 123 (Photodeti), 127 top (Elena Vasilieva), 127 bottom (Erik Lam), 128 (Kirill Vorobyev), 129 top (Judith Dzierzawa), 131 (Vladyslav Starozhylov), 132 (Linn Currie), 136 (Sergey Taran), 137 (Nikolai Tsvetkov), 138 (Dmitri Pravdjukov), 139 top (Erik Lam), 141 (Linn Currie), 142 (Natalyka), 143 (Linn Currie), 144 (Sarah Fields), 147 (Linn Currie), 149 top (Photodeti), 157 (Nelikz), 160 (Natalyka), 163 (Mariya Miftakhova), 202 top (Thomas Hertwig), 203 (Verastuchelova)

Dreamstime/Eric Isselee: 12, 14, 20, 27, 28, 40, 56, 74 bottom, 81, 95, 107, 115, 116, 125, 126, 130, 133, 139 bottom, 161, 194 top

Fotolia: 11 (Katerina Cherkaslina), 15 (Dixi), 89 bottom (Olhastock), 92 bottom (Eric Isselee), 96 (Chris Brignell), 98 top (Dixi), 105 bottom (Eric Isselee), 118 top (Kirill Vorobyev), 140 (Dixi)

Shutterstock: 9 (Schankz), 13 (Elena09), 17 (Schankz), 18 (Susan Schmitz), 21 top (Dora Zett), 21 bottom (Kanut Srinin), 22 (Yevgeniy11), 23 (Dorota Emilia), 24 (Wk1003mike), 25 (Okssi), 26 (Sergey Taran), 29 top (Dora Zett), 29 bottom (Stock SK), 30 (Denis Nata), 31 (Levant Konuk), 32 (Lifetime Stock), 33 (Alberto Duran Photography), 34 (Robynrg), 35 (Dora Zett), 36 (Eric Isselee), 38 (Oleksandr Lytvynenko), 39 (279 Photo Studio), 43 (Olhastock), 44 (Krissi Lundgren), 45 (Miras Wonderland), 46 (Grigory L), 47 (Chepko Danil Vitalevich), 48 (Olhastock), 49 (Uzhursky), 50 (Casey Christopher), 51 (Anneka), 52 top (David W Hughes), 52 bottom (Lana M), 53 (Helen Sushitskaya), 54 top (Africa Studio), 54 bottom (Lizard), 55 (Kanstantsin Navitski), 57 (Lana K), 58 top (Willie Cole), 59 (Cynoclub), 60 (Mark Wolters), 61 (Dora Zett), 62 top (Foryoui3), 62 bottom (Tony Campbell), 63 (Mara Ze), 64 (Cozy Nook), 65 (Alexander Ermolaev), 66 (Africa Studio), 67 (Panyawat Bootanom), 68 (Tony Campbell), 69 (Absolutimages), 70 (Tsekhmister), 71 top (Africa Studio), 71 bottom (Oleksandr Lytvynenko), 72 (Naisakorn), 73 (Olhastock), 74 (Tsekhmister), 75 (Rachel Moon), 76 (Lina Kiel), 77 (Oleksandr Lytvyneko), 78 & 79 top (Olhastock), 79 bottom (Oleksandr Lytvynenko), 80 both (Africa Studio), 82 top (Tony Campbell), 82 bottom (Olhastock), 83 (Africa Studio), 84 (Halfpoint), 85 (Anna Khomulo), 86 (Audrey Kuzmin), 87 (Anastasia Skorobogatova), 88 (Bruce Raynor), 89 top (Santypan), 90 (My Images – Micha), 91 (Anna Utekhina), 92 top (Oscar C Williams), 93 (Thosawat Chumchuen), 94 (Pelfophoto), 97 (Vladyslav Starozhylov), 100 (Sandra Huber), 101 (Gudz Sofiya), 102 (Alexander Ermolaev), 103 top (Vincent Noel), 103 bottom (Goodluz), 104 (Bmf-foto.de), 105 top (Elnur), 106 (Chomphucar), 108 (Susana Aires), 109 (Studio Peace), 111 (Alex James Bramwell), 112 (Jeremy Pidgeon), 113 (Bartkowski), 114 (Alexander Ermolaev), 122 (Africa Studio), 124 (Pakornkrit Khantaprab), 129 bottom (NE Studio), 134 (Budmir Jevtic), 135 (NE Studio), 145 (Sergey Kuznecov), 146 top (Elena Butinova), 146 bottom (Erik Lam), 148 (Artem Voropai), 149 bottom (Susan Schmitz), 150 (Zoran Photographer), 151 top (Natalia 7), 151 bottom (Schankz), 152 (Kucher Serhii), 153 (Jon Schulte), 154 top (Sheila Fitzgerald), 154 bottom (Anna Anderson Fotografi), 155 (Sinelev), 156 (Tsekhmister), 158 (Alexander Ermolaev), 159 top (Schankz), 159 bottom (Stock_SK), 161 (Gordana Sermek), 162 (Maja Marjanovic), 164 (Okssi), 165 (Somprathana Wapinanon), 166 & 167 top (Oleksandr Lytvynenko), 167 bottom (Bmf-foto.de), 168 (Lario), 169 (Africa Studio), 170 (Astrid Gast), 171 (Cynoclub), 172 top (Ekaterina Kolomeets), 172 bottom (Zrenjaninac), 173 (Susan Schmitz), 174 (Dora Zett), 175 top (Denis Nata), 175 bottom (Oleksandr Lytvynenko), 176 & 177 (Tony Campbell), 178 (Africa Studio), 179 top (Kostasgr), 179 bottom (Exopixel), 180 (Africa Studio), 181 (Anna Utekhina), 182 (Sari O'Neal), 183 (Veronika Kachalkina), 184 (Dora Zett), 185 top (Oleksandr Lytvynenko), 185 bottom (Yellow Cat), 186 (Willee Cole), 187 top (Dmitry Steshenko), 187 bottom (Borzywoj), 188 top (Africa Studio), 188 bottom (Tsekhmister), 189 (OKcamera), 190 (Grigory L), 191 top (Julie Vader), 191 (Dora Zett), 192 (Yellow Cat), 193 (Thaisign), 194 bottom (Tony Campbell), 195 (Megan Betteridge), 196 top (Elena Nichizhenova), 196 bottom (Cynoclub), 197 (Anurak Pongpatimet), 198 (Oksana Kuzmina), 199 (Renata Apanaviciene), 200 top (Wavebreakmedia), 200 bottom (Okssi), 201 & 202 bottom (Oksana Kuzmina)